WEAPON

THE BAZOOKA

GORDON L. ROTTMAN

Series Editor Martin Pegler

First published in Great Britain in 2012 by Osprey Publishing, Midland House, West Way, Botley, Oxford, OX2 0PH, UK

44-02 23rd Street, Suite 219, Long Island City, NY 11101, USA

E-mail: info@ospreypublishing.com

A CIP catalog record for this book is available from the British Library

Print ISBN: 978 1 84908 801 5

PDF ebook ISBN: 978 1 84908 802 2

ePub ebook ISBN: 978 1 78096 463 8

Page layout by Mark Holt

Index by Alison Worthington

Battlescene artwork by Johnny Shumate

Cutaways by Alan Gilliland

Typeset in Sabon and Univers

Originated by PDQ Media, Bungay, UK

Printed in China through Worldprint Ltd.

12 13 14 15 16   10 9 8 7 6 5 4 3 2 1

Osprey Publishing is supporting the Woodland Trust, the UK's leading woodland conservation charity, by funding the dedication of trees.

Editor's note

Bazookas were in use from 1942 through to the early 1970s. In this study, contemporary US customary linear measurements (in, ft, yd) and weights (oz, lb) will be used rather than metric. The following data will help comparing the US and metric measurements:

> 1yd = 0.9m
> 1ft = 0.3m
> 1in = 2.54cm/25.4mm
> 1lb = 0.45kg
> 1oz = 0.028kg

When a parenthesized "T" designation follows the "M" designation of a weapon or ammunition item, e.g., M30 (T127E3), the "T" is the trials designation of the standardized model. The armor penetration ability statistics of various projectiles quoted in this work are taken from official documents. The penetration is based on the projectile striking the armor at zero degrees under ideal conditions. The reality is that projectiles seldom strike at zero degrees either because of the angle of impact and/or the slope of the armor. They will actually penetrate less than what official documents claim. German weapons of 15mm and lesser caliber were designated in millimeters (mm). Larger-caliber weapons were designated in centimeters (cm).

Acknowledgements

The author is indebted to Frederick Adolphus of the Fort Polk Museum, LA; Jeff Hunt and Jean and Bob Gates of the Texas Military Forces Museum, Austin, TX; Edward Rudnicki, and Laurent Touchard for sharing reference materials; and Tom Laemlein of Armor Plate Press for his photographic support.

Abbreviations

AFV	armored fighting vehicle
AP	armor-piercing
fps	feet per second
HE	high-explosive
HEAT	high-explosive antitank (shaped charge)
HC	hexachloroethane (burning-type white screening smoke)
rpm	rounds per minute
R.PzB.	*Raketenpanzerbüchse* – rocket [anti-]armor gun
WP	white phosphorus (bursting-type white screening smoke and casualty-producing compound)

Cover images are courtesy author and Tom Laemlein/Armor Plate Press.

CONTENTS

INTRODUCTION

In January 1943, a Hauptmann Buchstein, Ic (intelligence officer) of 10. Panzer-Division, submitted a prisoner interrogation report describing a new American antitank weapon found in Tunisia. The prisoner, an NCO of the US 1st Armored Division, apparently willingly provided the description of a man-portable rocket launcher capable of destroying tanks. To the prisoner's credit, he gave a somewhat misleading description of the weapon's characteristics, either intentionally or through unfamiliarity. The weapon was, after all, new even to the Americans – regular troops did not know much more about it than the Germans. It had first been encountered by the Germans at Hill 295 near Medjez-el-Bab, Tunisia, the previous December; US and British troops had landed in Morocco and Algeria on November 8, 1942 in Operation *Torch*, and then advanced into Tunisia.

Hauptmann Buchstein wrote that the electrically fired rocket launcher was 1.2m (48in) long and consisted of a light steel tube with a caliber of "8cm" (3.2in). His description further stated that the weapon could be "fired by individual riflemen and reportedly has a tremendous armor breaking force." What Hauptmann Buchstein reported was officially known in US forces as the 2.36in M1 antitank rocket launcher, or more commonly, a "bazooka" or "stovepipe," of considerably smaller caliber than he was told. In German reports it was called the *Panzerbüchse* (armor-burster), the general term for an antitank rifle. Later the Germans would refer to captured M1 bazookas as the 6cm *Raketenpanzerbüchse* (R.PzB.) 788(a).

The bazooka, for its time, was an infantryman's dream come true. The beginning of World War II found many European armies equipped with mostly inadequate antitank weapons: small-caliber antitank guns, overly heavy antitank rifles, marginally effective antitank hand and rifle grenades, hand-emplaced antitank charges, and antitank mines. For the most part these weapons were too heavy, too cumbersome, too short-ranged, and/or largely impotent. Most were obsolete or obsolescent at best by 1940–41 as heavier, better-protected tanks and other armored fighting vehicles (AFVs) were fielded. Research agencies were soon searching for, even grasping at, any type of weapon and concept that might help defeat the improved AFVs. Some of these weapons were impractical, some were desperate, and some worked better than others. They ran the gamut from factory-produced Molotov cocktails to shoulder-fired rocket launchers, a comparatively new concept.

Antitank guns performed their role to varied degrees of success, but those issued to infantry units were too light, around 37mm (1.45in) caliber, which was only effective against the lightest AFVs. Even the small infantry antitank guns were difficult to conceal and time-consuming to move between firing positions, an essential tactic if they were to survive. Antitank rifles were even less effective, and because of their length and weight they were too heavy for the needs of foot-mobile infantry. They were also expensive. Only the Soviets were pleased with the antitank rifle, but it was

This staged photograph (the assistant gunner would not be so exposed) was taken in Normandy. It does demonstrate the preferred angle of attack on a Panzer PzKfw V, from the flank, as well as show what the HEAT rocket's detonation looks like. The bazookaman is armed with an M1A1. The assistant carries an empty M6 rocket bag on his left side. (Hulton Archive/Getty)

A 4th Infantry Division rifleman examines two German 8.8cm *Raketenpanzerbüchse* R.PzB. 54 "rocket [anti-]armor guns," also known as the *Ofenrohr* (stovepipe) or *Panzerschreck* (armor terror), in France, July, 1944. The one on the ground lacks the detachable blast shield, which was often removed in combat. It was almost twice as heavy as the M1A1 bazooka. (Tom Laemlein/Armor Plate Press)

by no means ideal. Antitank hand and rifle grenades were short-ranged and inaccurate, and offered poor armor penetration. Hand-thrown or hand-emplaced antitank charges, sometimes called hand-mines, were virtually suicide weapons and suffered the same limitations as hand grenades. Apart from armor-penetrating grenades, smoke and irritant gas (tear gas) grenades were available to blind tank crews. Antitank mines were strictly a defensive "hit or miss" means of slowing AFVs, and were time and manpower intensive to install. In fact, most antitank weapons were defensive in nature, even though they had application in offensive operations. True offensive antitank weapons had to be self-propelled mobile mounts with some degree of armor protection, i.e. tanks and tank destroyers.

Ideally, what infantrymen needed was a comparatively lightweight antitank weapon, no heavier than the squad's automatic weapon – the 20lb Browning Automatic Rifle (BAR) – and offering at least a 200yd range. It had to be reliable in all weather conditions, rugged enough for the rigors of combat, simple to operate, easy to train operators on, require only a small crew (two men) and be able to knock out at least medium tanks. It would be useful, too, for it to be capable of attacking other targets such as infantry field fortifications, defended buildings, crew-served weapons, and troops in the open, as well as being able to lay down screening smoke.

At the time though there was no such comprehensive requirement or specification for an infantry antitank weapon. The whole idea of a light, man-portable, lethal antitank weapon was relatively new. Most developers were chained to the limitations of conventional projectile-firing guns. The larger the caliber of the projectile and the higher its velocity (to achieve effective penetration) the larger and heavier the resulting weapon was. The weight and bulk, of course, limited mobility, a vital component in the ideal infantry antitank weapon.

In 1942 US Army and Marine Corps infantry units possessed inadequate antitank capabilities. The 37mm M3A1 antitank gun was found at battalion and regimental levels. Based on the principal German antitank gun, the Rheinmetall 3.7cm PaK 35/36 (PaK stands for *Panzerabwehrkanone* – antiarmor gun), the M3A1 was relatively light (950lb) for this type of gun and had a low profile of just 38in. It was fielded in early 1940 and remained in use through the war, although it began to be replaced by the 57mm M1 gun in 1944 (a copy of the British 6pdr). At 500yd the 37mm could penetrate 2.4in of armor with its armor-piercing (AP) round. It also had high-explosive (HE) and canister (antipersonnel via lead balls) ammunition. One deficiency of small-caliber antitank guns was they offered only a feeble HE round, limiting their utility for antipersonnel fire and attacking field fortifications. The Germans referred to their 3.7cm PaK as the *Türklopfer* (Doorknocker). The US "thirty-seven" was originally called the "little poison" owing to its accuracy and high velocity. That nickname was dropped once combat showed it was largely ineffective against newer tanks.

The United States was one of the few major powers entering the war without an antitank rifle. The beginning of World War II, however, found many European armies relying on antitank rifles as their primary infantry antitank weapons. In fact, the very first purpose-built antitank weapon had originated in World War I. In early 1918 the Germans fielded a massive single-shot, bolt-action, bipod-mounted Mauser antitank rifle, weighing 35.27lb, measuring 66.14in long, and in 13.2mm caliber. It was called the *Tank Abwehr Gewehr Mod. 18* (Tank Defense Rifle or T. Gew. – "T-rifle"). Subsequent European antitank rifles weighed between 29lb and 46lb, heavier than many machine guns. Their length varied from 43in to 64in so they were not exactly handy weapons. With a caliber of 7.9mm, 12.7mm, 0.55in (14mm), 14.5mm, or 20mm, they could generally penetrate only 0.78in or so of armor at a range between 110 and 330yd, *if* the bullet struck the tank at zero degrees. The main damage inflicted by the slug, if it managed to penetrate the armor, was to ricochet about the inside of the tank to take out crewmen. By 1940 the antitank rifle was obsolete owing to thicker, ballistically sloped armor. The weight and bulk of the "elephant guns" made them impractical for dismounted infantry operations, especially since the most effective method of attacking tanks was to stalk them. This tactic required the antitank rifle crew to sneak about using available cover and concealment and making fast rushes to gain advantageous firing positions, enabling them to attack tanks' rear and flanks.

By the time of the Korean War the 2.36in bazooka was ineffective against modern AFVs like the T-34/85, but the new 3.5in M20 "super-bazooka" could be devastating. Here, a Marine rocket gunner strides toward Seoul after the September 1950 Inch'on landing. He transports the M20 in the broken-down travel mode, demonstrating its ease of carry. All Marine units arrived in Korea armed with the new 3.5in. (Tom Laemlein/Armor Plate Press)

7

While the United States undertook some experimentation with antitank rifles, instead it initially used the Browning .50cal M2 machine gun in this role. While being a heavier and bulkier weapon than even the antitank rifle, it riddled light AFVs with AP rounds much more effectively than single rounds from a bolt-action antitank rifle (some antitank rifles were semi-automatic, making them weightier, more expensive, and temperamental). By the time the United States entered combat in December 1941, though, the .50cal had been withdrawn from this role and mainly used in an antiaircraft role, as it was now inadequate against armor.

By 1942 the only other US antitank weapon was the M9A1 antitank rifle grenade, the squad antitank weapon. The 1941 M9 had been copied from the German GG/P 40 and lacked the nose cone that would provide the standoff necessary for an effective shaped-charge projectile. To make matters worse, it had a nose fuse, further hampering the shaped-charge effect. (The German model had a base-detonating fuse.) The M9 was withdrawn and the 1942 M9A1 was issued with a nose cone and base-detonating fuse, allowing it to penetrate 3–4in under ideal conditions. Here was the first US use of the shaped-charge technology that would make the bazooka a viable antitank weapon. Until a dedicated launcher was available for the semi-automatic M1 Garand rifle in late 1943, squads used a bolt-action Springfield M1903 rifle for grenade launching. Initially there was one grenade launcher per squad, but by 1944 the Army was issuing two or three and the Marines issued one to every rifleman – although usually, not all were actually carried. Rifle grenades had only about a 100yd effective range against moving AFVs and were mainly used for attacking fighting positions and personnel. Coincidently, the antitank rifle grenade was the first use of the shaped charge by Germany, Britain, the USSR, and Japan.

Blinding smoke was effective for close combat against AFVs, making it difficult or impossible for AFV crews to detect attackers and targets, maneuver, and engage targets, as well as screening infantrymen moving in for close attack. Tanks operated in groups allowing them to protect one another from close attack. Dismounted infantry would also accompany AFVs for close protection. Smoke would also blind the accompanying tanks and infantry from the attackers.

Both the US Army and Marines issued the AN-M8 smoke grenade, M1 smoke pot, and M15 white phosphorus (WP) grenade. The M8 grenade and M1 smoke pot were burning-type pyrotechnics, but the M15 (issued at the end of 1943) was a bursting-type grenade that not only generated screening smoke, but blasted out burning casualty-producing WP gobs and particles that would burn through flesh.

Field-expedient means of attacking tanks such as Molotov cocktails, sticky bombs, satchel charges, shooting rifles at vision ports, tossing mines into the tracks, and climbing aboard to drop grenades in a hatch were means of last resort and certainly not something that could be relied on for effective antitank defense. Hence the infantry desperately needed a new type of antitank weapon, for which no complete requirement and specification existed. Such a weapon would not be available until a small number of officers began, to borrow a modern phrase, thinking outside the box.

DEVELOPMENT
An unlikely weapon

"The 'bazooka' ... came about in a rather devious fashion ..." said Col Leslie A. Skinner, father of the weapon. What the infantryman needed was simply the melding of two emerging technologies: the armor-penetrating shaped charge and the rocket motor. Granted, both the rocket and the shaped charge had been around for some time, but further development, innovative materials, and fresh ideas made them more effective and essentially new weapons.

The rocket had its origins in ancient China. Its use as a weapon, though disputed, goes back to AD 1232 when rockets were used against the Mongols. They saw limited use as barrage-firing weapons into the 1800s. They were also used for signaling. The inaccuracy and erratic flight of black-powder rockets limited their effectiveness, however. Pioneering work on the modern rocket was undertaken by the father of modern rocketry, Robert H. Goddard (1882–1945), prior to World War I. He developed designs for multistage and gyroscopic control rockets, and rockets propelled by liquid propellant. During World War I he proposed open-ended tube-type rocket launchers as infantry weapons. These rocket guns were 1in-, 2in-, and 3in-caliber "recoil-free" weapons launching 1.4lb, 8.5lb, and 16.5lb rockets, respectively. The launcher tube was 5ft 6in long for all three calibers. Goddard was unable to fabricate electrical firing systems in time for the November 1918 demonstrations at Aberdeen Proving Ground, MD, so he used simple match-lit fuses, as on fireworks. He also used a crude substitute propellant, but it was adequate enough to work effectively. One of the officers viewing the demonstration stated that it "could be developed to operate successfully against tanks." Even at that early date and despite the fact that Germany fielded only a couple of dozen tanks, the weapon's need was appreciated. The spectators were impressed,

9

Capt Edward G. Uhl, one of the principal designers of the bazooka, demonstrates the 2.36in T1 rocket launcher used in the Aberdeen Proving Ground demonstration in May 1942. The considerably longer T1 was re-engineered and adopted as the M1 antitank rocket launcher on June 24, 1942. The T1's tube was longer than the M1's; it lacked the connect box atop the tube and an effective sight, and had crude handgrips and a shoulder stock made from an old rifle stock. (US Army)

but the Armistice occurred just days later and no further research was undertaken.

The US Army showed little interest in rockets or any other unusual weapon until 1933, when the Ordnance Department established a Rocket Branch to examine the potential of powered missiles. The "branch" consisted of one man, then-Capt Leslie A. Skinner (1902–88). Many conventionally minded Ordnance officers shunned the rocket concept. Skinner built his own rockets prior to World War I, but his hobby was unappreciated when, in 1915, one of his devilish contrivances set the post hospital's roof on fire; his father was an Army surgeon at the same hospital. During the 1920s he graduated from West Point and was commissioned in the Army Air Corps. Skinner transferred to the Ordnance Department in 1931. On his own he developed aircraft rockets, inspired by the 1918 report on Goddard's rocket tubes, and conducted more than 200 test launches. Skinner remained with the Rocket Branch until reassigned to Hawaii in 1938.

THE BIRTH OF THE BAZOOKA

With the start of the war in 1939, the US Army was studying battlefield reports from Europe. The threat of massed German armor and *Blitzkrieg* tactics prompted a reappraisal of antitank tactics and weapons, resulting in an increase of antitank guns allocated to infantry units and the establishment of the Tank Destroyer Command at the end of 1941. The Army had stated the requirement for a recoilless grenade launcher in 1940. The specifications have not survived, unfortunately, other than they required a shaped-charge projectile. The need for a recoilless rocket launcher was apparent, as heavy conventional projectiles tended to damage the small arms attempting to launch them.

Dr Clarence N. Hickman (1889–1987), a researcher at Clark University, Worcester, MA, who had worked with Goddard in 1918, was in charge of Section H (Investigations on Propulsion) of the National Defense Research Committee (NDRC), which had been organized to coordinate, supervise, and conduct scientific research on the development, production, and use of mechanisms and devices of warfare. In 1941 he proposed the continuation of Goddard's rocket tube development as a means of delivering a warhead capable of piercing a battleship's deck. The US Navy was not interested, however, preferring an aircraft rocket. This is often misinterpreted as having been a rejected proposal for the bazooka. However, development of the 3.5in air-to-ground rocket resulted and should not be confused with the later 3.5in super bazooka. (The 3.5in air-to-ground rocket was canceled in preference for the 5in.)

The British undertook rocket experimentation in the 1930s and fielded antiaircraft rockets prior to World War II, which they designated with the cover name of "Unrotated Projectiles" (UPs). The development of the 2in and 3in antiaircraft rockets was completed by mid-1940 and they were used from 1941. The 2in rocket was fitted aboard merchant ships, while the 3in was mounted aboard warships. The 2in rockets were launched from Mk II "Pillar Box" rack-type projectors holding 20 rockets. With the decline of the convoy air threat, the "Pillar Boxes" were removed in 1942. They reemerged in 1944, being set up on the British coast to engage V1 flying bombs.

Dr Hickman, being familiar with Skinner's work, requested his reassignment to help pursue the recoilless antitank gun project. He was assigned to Navy Powder Factory, Indian Head, MA, to establish the Army Special Projects Unit to co-develop rockets with the Navy. In September 1940 the Ordnance Department purchased British 2in rockets and a single "Pillar Box." The 2in antiaircraft rocket, while being examined in detail by the bazooka's developers, was not copied or adapted for the bazooka's 2.36in missile. The 10.75lb 2in rocket had a straight 3ft-long tubular body, blunt-nosed 2.5lb HE warhead, and four blade fins, and was actually 2.25in in diameter. It was fitted with a self-destruct fuse that detonated at 4,500ft. Without the self-destruct feature it could reach 10,000ft.

Yet one point learned from testing 2in rockets was that the single-grain propellant (solid propellant charge) was too slow-burning. The rocket propellant had to burn instantaneously, almost as fast as the propellant detonation of a conventional cartridge antitank gun. The projectile needed an immediate high-velocity boost and the propellant needed to burn completely by the time it left the comparatively short launch tube. The 2in rocket propellant burned for 1.2 seconds, of which only 0.1 second was before the rocket actually launched. If the propellant completely ignited in the tube the resulting missile flight would be more accurate, rather than suffering from even tiny flight deviation if the propellant was still burning outside the tube. In addition, the operator would not be endangered by still-burning propellant being blown back on him from beyond the muzzle.

Undertaking M1A1 bazooka training at Fort Benning, GA, in September, 1943. The rocket's back-blast is readily demonstrated. Even though the muzzle cannot be seen, it is apparent that there is no muzzle flash, as the propellant was completely ignited before the rocket left the muzzle. There was a complete absence of recoil. (Tom Laemlein/Armor Plate Press)

Another project, at that time unrelated to rockets, was the M10 high-explosive antitank (HEAT) grenade.[1] The basic design was developed by Henry H. Mohaupt (1915–2001), a young Swiss Army machine-gunner and largely self-educated engineer. When he demonstrated his shaped-charge design in 1940, the US Army was skeptical of his claims. In fact, it performed very well and the Germans were already using it in rifle grenades and large demolition charges. The 30mm shaped-charge antitank rifle grenade was tested by the Ordnance Department and found capable of penetrating 2in of armor. The Army also received an intelligence report from the British stating the Germans were moving to 4in frontal armor on newer tanks, so the M10 grenade was developed further to penetrate this.

The M10 HEAT was a spigot grenade (i.e. having a tailboom that slid over a launcher tube on the rifle's muzzle) with a shaped-charge warhead along the lines of the M9A1 antitank rifle grenade. The warhead itself was 2.36in caliber and 8.8in long, and weighed 1.57lb. (The actual caliber was 2.365in and the later launchers' bore was 2.37in.) Different launchers were tested, including various spigot mortars and even "rifle grenade"-type launchers fitted on .50cal M2 machine guns and M1903 Springfield

---

[1] At the time the HEAT (today pronounced "heat") round was known as the HE, AT and pronounced "H-E-A-T." The modern HEAT abbreviation is used in this book.

rifles. Assorted tailbooms and fins were fitted depending on the type of launcher.

All of these launchers fired their projectiles at a high angle in order to achieve satisfactory range. They lacked sufficient velocity for the flat-trajectory fire that was so essential for engaging maneuvering tanks. The high-angle trajectory resulted in wide dispersion of projectiles and the heavy recoil damaged machine guns and rifles – it even broke rifle stocks when placed on the ground to absorb the recoil.

The spigot mortars attempted to drop rounds onto the target. This approach made sense, as tanks' top armor was thinner, but it had as much chance of hitting even a slow-moving tank as firing a conventional mortar at it. Another problem with the spigot mortars was that they were difficult for infantrymen to carry and set up – a tank could not be stalked with a spigot mortar. No description exists of these mortars, which were offered by five different manufacturers. The M10 shaped-charge projectile therefore held promise, but there was no effective means of delivering it.

Leslie Skinner later wrote: "The number of 'inventors' of the bazooka has fallen and risen as troubles developed and were cured, the stage having been reached in one part of its career where only those who worked on it could be found to claim any connection to it." As far back as December 1940, Skinner showed a sketch of an electrically ignited, tube-type shoulder-fired rocket launcher to Gregory J. Kessenich, chief of the Ordnance Department's Patent Section, who was familiar with rocket patents. What was lacking was a suitable armor-penetrating warhead. Skinner was told there was no interest in such a weapon. That thinking was short-lived, for in April 1941 Kessenich let slip to Skinner that a new type of warhead was under development. This was the M10 HEAT grenade.

Through the early months of 1941 Skinner worked on and off on the fast-burning double-base powder propellant rocket motor in his basement workshop. The first crude test-firings were conducted in May. In June, Skinner's Special Projects Unit was doubled in size by the addition of 2nd Lt Edward G. Uhl (pronounced "Yule"; 1918–2010), a recent engineering physics graduate. With a minimal budget and limited resources, Skinner worked on aircraft and artillery rockets while Uhl concentrated on antitank rockets. Uhl worked with his Navy counterparts, exchanging assistance and ideas. The young officer also worked on the launcher tube and conducted further test firings. Col Hickman continued to provide advice. In the early spring of 1942, Lt Col Wiley T. Moore, chief of the Engineering Group of the Small Arms Division, saw the

A case of ten 2.36in T1 antitank rockets, June 1942. The T1 became the M6 HEAT rocket. The T1s and early M6s were all-yellow with black markings. Later M6-series HEAT rounds were olive drab with yellow markings for camouflage purposes. Standard packaging was 20-round boxes.
(Tom Laemlein/Armor Plate Press)

possibilities of the new weapon concept. He paved the way for Frankfort Arsenal, PA, to produce the first test launcher and the parts to mate the rocket motors and M10 HEAT projectile.

Kessenich also designed a rocket prototype, which was somewhat different from the final design adopted for the bazooka. It contained the shaped charge in the front half of the warhead with what would have been an ineffective nose fuse and the rocket motor in the rear with the fins attached to the rear end. There was no tailboom containing the motor. (As a side note, Kessenich could not patent his bazooka rocket design as it was classified "Top Secret." In May 1941 he was commissioned a colonel, but as a civilian employee he was entitled to royalties under certain circumstances. This was protested by the Army and taken to court after the war. He was granted patent 2,579,323 in 1951 and in 1962 his estate was granted $100,000 by the US government.)

By May 1942 Skinner and now-Capt Uhl had a reasonably reliable rocket and launcher. They used a 5ft 5in-long steel tube, found in a scrapheap, that accepted the 2.36in M10 warhead. Skinner donated an old spare wooden rifle stock for the shoulder rest and recommended a pair of wooden handgrips be attached. The rear handgrip was fitted with a trigger that activated the electrical igniter. A lead wire connected the trigger to a wire protruding from the rocket's nozzle. There was no sighting system, as up to this point they had only fired inert rockets into the Potomac River, not attempting to hit a target. Uhl initially wore a welder's mask and gloves to protect him from burning propellant. Surprisingly, in a display of supreme confidence, Uhl fired the launcher from his shoulder at its first test-firing rather than a safer remote static firing. He reported that upon firing he heard a loud whoosh and felt absolutely no recoil. The first test shot demonstrated the protective gear was unnecessary, as the test launcher's tube was longer than the production model, ensuring that all the propellant was ignited in the tube. The weapon was at the time referred to with the codename "Whip."

Skinner deemed that the rocket and launcher were ready for a test. In May 1942, such a test was scheduled at Aberdeen Proving Ground, where five different makes of spigot mortars for launching the M10 HEAT round would be demonstrated to the Army Ground Forces. Although not on the schedule, Skinner and Uhl traveled to Aberdeen to demonstrate the weapon, technically going absent without informing their superiors of their intent and destination. On the morning of the test, the chief of the Ordnance Department's Technical Staff, Brig Gen Gladeon M. Barnes, was present. A group of officers arrived headed by Lt Gen Lesley McNair, Commanding General, Army Ground Forces. An M3 medium tank was on-hand and would run a prescribed course at 25mph as inert M10 rounds were fired at it. Uhl, learning the speed and range from the driver, did some quick calculations on a matchbook cover and determined he needed to aim one tank length in front and slightly above the turret top. The launcher still lacked a sight, so Uhl rapidly fashioned one from a broken nail and bent clothes hanger wire. It was bore-sighted using a telephone pole as an aim point – hardly an effectively calibrated sight for such an important test.

Capt Uhl shoulders an early 2.36in M1 antitank rocket launcher during a June 1942 ordnance display. This early model has a front sight frame on both sides of the muzzle and the pivoting rear sight meant it could be fired from either shoulder. Production models had reconfigured sights, allowing only right-shoulder firing. It can be seen here that the fore handgrip was unnecessary and it was deleted from the M1A1. (US Army)

Each of the five spigot mortars fired several inert rounds in turn at the moving tank. Every one of the relatively slow-moving, high-trajectory rounds missed, prompting groans from the audience. It was a dismal performance. These spigot mortars are described as having a solid rod onto which the hollow tailboom slid to point upward at an angle. A trigger mechanism was fitted at the base of the rod. Pressing the trigger released a firing pin in the top of the rod and this ignited the propellant in the grenade's base to launch it. The recoil was absorbed by the ground. They were said to be light, compact, and easy to operate. No photographs or illustrations have been found.

The sixth firing position was occupied by Skinner and Uhl. There were some sour expressions and groans when they unveiled the crude-looking tube and nine rockets. It barely looked like a weapon. Uhl shouldered the tube, took aim at the moving tank, and launched the rocket to score a first-round hit. The stunned crowd cheered and Lt Gen McNair asked Skinner if he could fire the strange weapon. Not to be outdone, Brig Gen Barnes fired a rocket as did several others with only one miss. After all nine rockets were expended, Barnes further examined the launcher and mentioned that, "It sure looks like Bob Burns' bazooka." The "bazooka" nickname stuck, but the first soldiers to use it in North Africa were not aware of what would become a legendary nickname.

The following week Gen George C. Marshall, Army Chief of Staff, was present for a formal demonstration at Camp Simms south of Washington, DC. He was accompanied by British and Soviet delegations. What was now the 2.36in T1 antitank rocket launcher was still a crude prototype. The demonstration impressed Marshall to the point that he immediately ordered 5,000 launchers with 25,000 rockets for Britain and the USSR under Lend-Lease, to be delivered within a month. General Electric in Bridgeport, CT was given the order on May 20, 1942.

The origin of the bazooka's nickname

After the May 1942 introductory demonstration firing of Skinner/Uhl's antitank rocket launcher, chief of the Ordnance Department's Technical Staff, Brig Gen Gladeon M. Barnes, noted the weapon's similarity to a farcical musical instrument called the "bazooka." This instrument was created by radio comedian and musician Bob Burns (1890–1956), the "Arkansas Traveler." He invented the trombone-like instrument in 1905, making it from two telescoping lengths of gas pipe and a whiskey funnel, and copyrighted it in 1920 (a smaller version was called the "kazooed bazooka"). The bazooka nickname was applied and stuck to what became the M1 rocket launcher. GIs frequently referred to the M1 launcher as a "zooka" and in the early days it was occasionally called the "shoulder 75," alluding to its having the power of a 75mm howitzer. The bazooka was also called the "stovepipe" for obvious reasons, and the *Ofenrohr* (stovepipe) nickname was also used by the Germans for their similar, but larger, 8.8cm R.PzB. 43 rocket launcher, the concept of which they copied from the 2.36in bazooka. Its official designation was *Raketenpanzerbüchse* (rocket [anti-]armor gun – *Büchse* is an old German term for a gun) and it bore another nickname of *Panzerschreck* (lit. "armor terror" – what it was hoped to inflict).

The concept of the post-World War II 3.5in M20-series "super bazooka" came from this German weapon. The term "super bazooka" soon fell from use once the 3.5in replaced the 2.36in to become just another "bazooka," or simply the "three-point-five." "Bazooka" is sometimes used loosely, and often incorrectly, to describe any form of small shoulder-fired rocket launcher or even recoilless rifle, especially by the lay media, which cannot seem to differentiate between rocket launchers and recoilless rifles. As Pfc Reed Brooks, a Korean War infantryman, commented, "Just like you did not call your rifle a gun, you did not call a 3.5in Rocket Launcher a bazooka, at least not in the drill sergeant's presence."

ABOVE Bob Burns, his instruments and an officer with a bazooka at Fort Hood, TX. (US Army)

A question is, how did Bob Burns come up with the name? This is not known. One theory is that it was derived from "bazoo," a now outdated term for a "windy fellow," a BS'er. There was also the term "palooka," identifying an incompetent athlete, especially a boxer, or a clumsy or slow-witted person. The word appeared in the 1920s. "Bazooka" Burns, by the way, conducted USO show tours entertaining servicemen during World War II accompanied by his original bazooka. Another fact that many are not aware of is that he joined the Marine Corps in World War I, making sergeant in the 11th Marines, and served as the Marines' jazz band conductor after the war.

THE 2.36in M1 ANTITANK ROCKET LAUNCHER

Ordnance engineers revised the weapon's design, adapting it to production requirements, improving the firing system, refining the sights, and shortening the tube. HEAT and practice rockets had to be designed for mass production. Much of the allotted time was spent making a working model that was approved by Ordnance. The fourteenth prototype was approved and only eight days remained to make the production run. Manning the makeshift production line with workers from other departments, office staff, and executives, the deadline was met with 89 minutes to spare. The stained shoulder stocks were not yet dry when they were packed. The Ordnance Committee type-classified (standardized) the modified version as the 2.36in M1 antitank rocket launcher and the rocket as the M6 HEAT on June 24, 1942. Series production was delayed

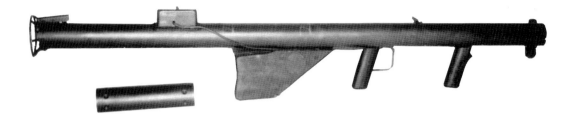

the first month, as steel tubing could not be obtained and there were minor design problems. The rockets were produced by the E.G. Budd Company of Philadelphia, PA, which normally built automobile bodies and stainless-steel railroad cars. In all, 112,790 M1s were produced.

The M1 bazooka was extremely simple, allowing low-cost rapid production. These factors also made it easy to repair, or it could simply be discarded if seriously damaged. The M1 was designed to be fired from either shoulder, but this facility was later deemed a non-essential feature and was dropped from later-production M1s and all other models, which could be fired from the right shoulder only. The front sight, graduated from 100yd to 400yd at 100yd intervals, was a frame-type sight on both sides (left side only on later production) of the muzzle. The rear peep sight, located one-quarter of the tube's length from the muzzle, could be swiveled left or right.

The launcher had two wooden handgrips, the rearward with the trigger protected by a trigger guard large enough to allow two-finger activation while wearing gloves. There was no accommodation for a shoulder sling. Some of the first production examples had a crude, folding but non-adjustable bipod just forward of the front handgrip. The wooden shoulder stock was fitted at the tube's midpoint. It contained the battery and a spare battery in the hasp-type trapdoor compartment on the stock's bottom. The battery was an Eveready 791-A, actually two standard "C" cell flashlight batteries in a cardboard tube. It could be substituted by two separate BA-42 batteries, the Army's designation for "C" cells.

A production M1 bazooka without the ambidextrous front and rear sights. The face guard added to M1 bazookas, seen below the tube, was snapped on over the shoulder stock. It protected the user's face from tube heat. (Tom Laemlein/Armor Plate Press)

The M1 bazooka is demonstrated. It possesses the ambidextrous front and rear sights. The connector box can be seen over the gunner's shoulder. Its lever on its rear is set to "Fire," the raised position. The connector latch atop the breech holds the rocket in place. This bazooka is not loaded; if it were, the rocket's fins would be seen. (Hulton Archive/Getty)

An Eveready 791-A, consisting of two standard "C" cell flashlight batteries in a cardboard tube, is removed from an M1's shoulder stock compartment. This is actually the spare battery. The connected battery is being held in place by this 29th Infantry Division gunner's finger in the rearmost of the two battery compartments. (Tom Laemlein/Armor Plate Press)

Contained in the forward upper portion of the stock was a circular compartment for the electrical system and a red indicator light on the left side. The light illuminated when the trigger was pressed to show a positive contact. A spare indicator light bulb was under the compartment's access plate. At three-quarters of the way along the tube's length was the connector box. One of the two wires of the electrical leads was grounded to the launcher and the other ran to the connector box then to the tail latch atop the breech. The box contained a lever to set it in Safe (down for loading) and Fire (up) positions – it dropped to Safe when the rocket was fired. The tail latch held the rocket in the breech and made the electrical connection to the rocket's fins. The connector box was removed from all M1s by field modification in July 1943, and spring-like contact coils were added, one on each side just forward of the breech. This allowed the lead wire protruding from the rocket nozzle to be coiled around either of the contact coils for ignition of the new M6A1 rockets. A wire frame guard encircled the breech. On rare occasions rocket motors detonated in the tube, blowing it apart with horrendous results for the operator – a problem lessened with the introduction of the improved M6A1 rocket. Reinforcing piano wire was therefore tightly wrapped around the tube's rear portion from the stock almost to the breech on late-production M1s, a feature included on subsequent models. All models of 2.36in bazooka were shipped in wooden crates containing six launchers.

THE 2.36in M1A1 ANTITANK ROCKET LAUNCHER

Naturally any weapon rushed through development on a shoestring budget, especially one devised without official sanction and support, would include shortcomings. Remedies to the various flaws and weaknesses were incorporated into a new model developed by the Ordnance Department through 1942 and into 1943. The 2.36in M1A1 antitank rocket launcher was type-classified on July 5, 1943. It would be several months before it saw combat duty. The M1A1 outwardly resembled the M1, but had a front sight on only the left muzzle and was now more realistically graduated from 100yd to 300yd; a folding rear peep sight replaced the ambidextrous swiveling sight. The stock and battery system were unchanged. A face guard was pressed on the upper portion of the tube above the stock – this protected the firer's face from barrel heat. As with late-production M1s, piano wire was wound around the rear portion of the tube for protection against premature rocket detonation. Contact coils for the rocket's lead wire were on either side of the breech along with the contact latch and breech guard. The former contact box was deleted and there was no safety lever. Fittings for a standard M1 web sling were mounted on the handgrip and to an attachment three-quarters of the way back from the muzzle. An 8in-diameter conical screen flash deflector was fitted to the muzzle. It prevented unburnt rocket propellant from being blown back in the firer's face. As it snagged on vegetation and other obstructions, the deflector was often removed, or else lost or knocked off in foliage. The M1A1's modifications improved performance, safety, and ease of use. However, only 59,932 M1A1s were produced, about half the number of M1s. M1s modified for the M6A1 rockets and other alterations remained in use. The modified M1s and all subsequent models could not fire the original M6 rockets.

THE 2.36in M9 ROCKET LAUNCHER

Other improvements and changes discovered through testing and combat reports made further modifications necessary. In November 1942, the Airborne Command stated the requirement for a "folding bazooka," as the 4ft 5in-long M1 and M1A1 were difficult to attach to paratroopers for airborne deployments. The solution was a two-piece tube connected by a three-lug interrupted-thread coupling. The ability to break down the launcher tube to half its length also made it easier to carry the bazooka through dense foliage, and made it practical for troops operating in jungles, mountains, and other rough terrain. It could also be more easily stowed in vehicles – in the travel mode it was only 31.5in long. Another benefit was that it allowed for a longer overall tube to increase range and accuracy; an assembled launcher was almost a man's height.

The development of the T21, T21E1, and T21E2 resulted in the 2.36in M9 rocket launcher, type-classified in June 1943. Note that "antitank" was no longer included in the designations of the M9 and later bazookas, the omission emphasizing the weapon's multitude of uses. The need for bazookas was such that M1A1 production could not be halted for M9 retooling. It took time for the much-revised M9 to enter production and reach the field, the earliest examples arriving in August 1944. Perfecting a reliable rigid coupling slowed progress, and then new production lines had to be set up and the weapon fed into the distribution pipeline. The M9 was only about 2.5lb heavier than its predecessor, and this was an acceptable tradeoff for a weapon that had a 50yd-better range and was capable of twice the rate of fire. It was also more accurate, more reliable, and more compact in the travel mode. Distribution priority went to airborne units and units in the Pacific.

The M1/M1A1's two-cell battery had proved to be an unreliable ignition system and did not generate sufficient charge at 14°F and below. In such cold weather, batteries were carried in inner pockets to keep them warm. On the M9 and later bazookas, batteries were replaced by a more reliable magneto inside the handgrip. This consisted of several magnets housing a coiled wire, which housed a steel armature. When the trigger was squeezed the armature rotated the coil and generated an electrical current. When triggered it generated a stronger electrical charge than the

battery packs. It was more resistant to temperature extremes, moisture, and tropical fungus corrosion, nor did it lose its charge over time.

THE 2.36in M9A1 ROCKET LAUNCHER

Barrel coupling problems continued and the M9 was strengthened by forging the nut portion rather than using stamped reinforcements. This modification resulted in the T9E1, type-classified as the 2.36in M9A1 rocket launcher in April 1944. The M9A1 was identical to the M9 other than in the barrel coupling design; the coupling's dimensional changes prevented interchangeability of front and rear barrel sections between the M9 and M9A1, and "M9A1" was stamped in white beside the forward barrel section's coupling. Fewer M9s were made than any other 2.36in version, other than the M18. Only 26,087 M9s were produced, as against 277,819 M9A1s. M9/M9A1s were produced by General Electric, but in July 1944 Cheney Bigelow Wire Works in Springfield, MA, was contracted and produced 40,000 M9A1s. Cheney Bigelow M9A1 serial numbers commenced with CB200001, while GE serial numbers had no prefix letters. M9A1 production commenced in September 1944, by both firms.

The M9/M9A1's forward barrel section had a conical muzzle-flash deflector, a barrel-latch strike behind the muzzle, and a barrel hook just forward of the rear end. These served to latch the forward barrel section to the rear section for carrying. The rear barrel section included the firing system and sight. The two sections were joined together via a three-lug interrupted thread coupling screw on the forward section. This was inserted into the barrel coupling nut on the forward end of the rear section and turned 60 degrees to lock it in place. To uncouple the barrel, the operator released the barrel coupling lock lever on the right side above the handgrip. The handgrip (with plastic grips) and the trigger were just behind the coupling, and the two-finger trigger was protected by an oversize trigger guard allowing even a mitten-covered hand to fire the weapon. The safety lever was on the upper rear of the handgrip – "Safe" (up), "Fire" (down) – and the firing magneto was contained inside the grip. An M1 web sling was attached to the bottom of the handgrip and below the breech guard.

The sight was fitted on the left side just to the rear of the handgrip (there was no longer a front sight). Early-production M9/M9A1s had the T43 folding bar sight mounted on a bracket plate. The 8.25in-long bar had a small stud for the front sight and a peep sight on the rear. A range indicator pointer allowed the estimated range to be set. The range scale was marked at 50yd intervals from 0yd to 600yd. When set for firing, the bar sight extended past the barrel coupling, and when broken down for transport it was pivoted to the rear on its double-jointed mounting. The hinged bar sight was easily knocked out of alignment in combat and proved inaccurate. The T90 optical reflecting ring sight was fitted to M9A1s made after September 1944. This sight could be mounted on existing launchers without modification to the sight bracket. It could be folded closed with the eyepiece against the launcher tube. The sight was non-magnifying and graduated with the same range scale as the bar sight.

Rather than a wooden stock, a shaped metal strap provided a two-position shoulder rest. Some had a simpler one-position rest. There were barrel latches and a release handle just behind the handgrip and at the breech end on the tube's right side. Wire reinforcing was wrapped around the barrel from the sight to the contact springs. A protected electrical wire ran from the handgrip back to the contact springs, one on either side of the tube just forward of the connector latch. The connector latch was atop of the breech, on which was a heavy wire breech guard.

THE 2.36in M18 ROCKET LAUNCHER

The final 2.36in bazooka was the 2.36in M18 rocket launcher. It was developed as the T90 to be type-classified in April 1945. While outwardly similar to the M9A1 and operated in exactly the same manner, most of its components were not interchangeable. Neither of the barrel sections was interchangeable with the M9A1's. "M18" was stamped in white on the

An assembled 2.36in M9 rocket launcher, this one a late model with the optical reflex sight rather than the crude bar sight. (Author, courtesy of Texas Military Forces Museum)

rear end of the front barrel and the front end of the rear barrel. The main difference was that the barrel was aluminum; this material prevented rusting, reduced maintenance, and cut the weight by 5.57lb, a considerable saving. The muzzle deflector, barrel-latch strike and hooks, barrel coupling nut and screw, sight bracket, and breech guard were steel fittings riveted or screwed to the barrel. Rather than a wire breech guard, the M18 had a short conical guard, which helped guide the rocket into the breech. It retained the wire reinforcing on the rear barrel and had a redesigned one-position shoulder stock. The optical reflecting sight was unchanged, but a rubber eyepiece was added. Many of the M18's features would be incorporated into the future "super bazooka."

M18 production was begun late in the war by General Electric and only 500 were made before the contract was cancelled, along with all other bazooka contracts, following VJ-Day. It is reported that 350 were sent to the Pacific for combat testing, probably in the Philippines and/or on Okinawa. It is not known if they arrived in time to see combat. If the war had continued the M18 would have been used in the invasion of Japan. Possibly some may have seen Korean service. M18 production was not resumed owing to the adoption of the super bazooka a month after World War II ended.

The aluminum-tubed 2.36in M18 rocket launcher was standardized in April 1945. It was 5.57lb lighter than the steel-tubed M9. Only 500 were made and 350 sent to the Pacific for combat testing in 1945. Besides the aluminum barrel, it had a simplified one-position shoulder rest. (US Army)

2.36in rocket launchers

Model	Weight	Length	Travel length	Effective range	Rate of fire
M1	13.1lb	54.5in	same	250yd	4–5rpm
M1A1	13.2lb	54.5in	same	250yd	4–5rpm
M9/M9A1	15.87lb	61in	31.5in	300yd	10rpm
M18	10.3lb	60.5in	31.5in	300yd	10rpm

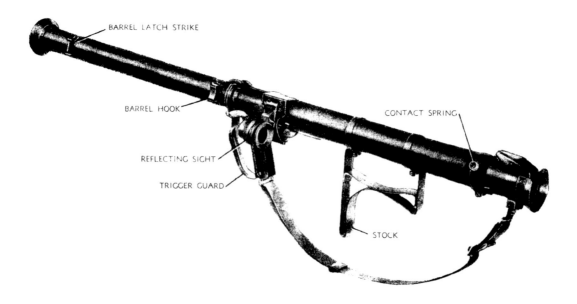

BARREL LATCH STRIKE

BARREL HOOK

REFLECTING SIGHT

TRIGGER GUARD

CONTACT SPRING

STOCK

Panzerschreck – the German bazooka

The Germans began development of their version of the bazooka in early 1943 based on examples of the M1 bazooka captured on the Eastern Front. The Germans opted for a larger caliber of 8.8cm (3.46in). The *Raketenpanzerbüchse* (R.PzB.) 43 (rocket [anti-]armor gun) was also known as the *Ofenrohr* (stovepipe) or *Panzerschreck*. This shoulder-fired weapon used a magneto firing system. It was 65in long and weighed 20.9lb, almost twice as heavy as the M1A1 bazooka. Its range was 150m (165yd). It was rugged, portable, low-cost, and large numbers could be produced rapidly; its production run was from November 1943 to February 1944.

The almost identical R.PzB.54 was adopted on August 12, 1944, accompanied by an improved rocket with a 180m (197yd) range. The new launcher weighed 24.2lb because of a shield protecting the gunner from muzzle-flash blowback – previously gunners had had to wear gloves and a gasmask with the filter removed. The Germans even issued rockets with different propellant for winter use, when the propellent burned more slowly, to reduce the blowback problem. The R.PzB.43 could not fire the new rocket and was reissued to second-line units. Only a small number of R.PzB.54s were produced before the R.PzB.54/1 was adopted on December 20, 1944, with a tube shortened by 5.25in (52.48in overall length) and its weight reduced to the former 20.9lb. It was not as accurate as its American counterpart but had about the same penetration as US 2.36in rockets. The 82nd Airborne Division's Reconnaissance Platoon fired a *Panzerschreck* and an M9 bazooka at a knocked-out Tiger II. The glacis armor was 6in. Both weapons penetrated to only 4in, but both were able to penetrate the 3.1in hull and turret side armor.

The R.PzB.54/1 was the most common model, with almost 290,000 of all versions produced along with 2,218,400 rockets. Regimental antitank gun companies were replaced by *Panzerzerstörer* (armor destroyer) companies, with 54 *Panzerschrecken* deployed in three platoons, each with 18 launchers in three squads. This provided a platoon to each of the infantry regiment's three battalions. They were normally employed in twos and threes, each weapon manned by a two-man crew, with overlapping fields of fire. Most units received fewer launchers, though.

ABOVE A soldier of the 83rd Infantry Division compares the German R.PzB.54/1 *Panzerschreck* with the M1A1 bazooka. Even the shortened *Panzerschreck* was still almost twice as heavy as the bazooka, and though of much larger caliber, both weapons had the same armor penetration. (Tom Laemlein/Armor Plate Press)

BELOW A German 8.8cm *Raketenpanzerbüchse* R.PzB.43, the original *Panzerschreck*, which first saw use in Italy in early 1944. The *Panzerschrecken* were heavier, less accurate, and shorter-ranged than the bazookas and achieved about the same armor penetration, about 4in. (Author)

THE SUPER BAZOOKA – THE 3.5in ROCKET LAUNCHERS

In 1943, development of the 3.25in T16 rocket launcher began in order to provide a weapon with greater armor penetration. (The T16 is not to be confused with the 3.25in M2 AA target rocket.) No records remain of this weapon's details and it may have been based on the mono-tube M1A1. With the development of the two-piece tube M9 series and the aluminum-tube M18, work on a new design was undertaken in October 1944, the 3.5in T74 launcher capable of penetrating 11in of armor. The scaling up of the caliber *may* have been influenced by the German 8.8cm *Panzerschreck*, which appeared in Italy in early 1944 and saw wider use on all fronts after the Normandy landings.

The weapons tagged the "super bazooka" were type-classified on October 11, 1945, as the 3.5in M20 and M20B1 rocket launchers. However, they would not enter limited production until 1948 and mass production until August 1950. The M9A1 and possibly some M18s saw combat in Korea, but proved to be ineffective against North Korean T-34/85 tanks with their well-sloped armor. The new 3.5in M20 super bazooka quickly replaced the 2.36in weapons and improved versions – the 3.5in M20A1 and M20A1B1 rocket launchers – were adopted in 1952.

The M20 and M20A1 were the two basic versions of the "three-point-five." Each was also available in a substitute model, the M20B1 and M20A1B1 respectively, which were adopted at the same time as their basic versions. (The "B" suffix designation indicated the use of a different manufacturing technique or substitute materials – both in the case of the M20 series.) The forward and rear aluminum barrels were interchangeable between all four models. On the M20 and M20A1, the muzzle deflector, breech guard, barrel couplings, barrel-latch strike and hook, monopod

Texas Army National Guardsmen of the 49th Armored Division demonstrate firing the M20A1B1 bazooka in the early 1960s. In training the gunner placed his hand atop his helmet to indicate the weapon was on "Safe" and his hand was clear of the trigger. It was taught, however, that this procedure was unnecessary in combat. (Texas Military Forces Museum)

bracket, and sight-mounting bracket were fastened by screws to the barrel sections. On the M20B1 and M20A1B1 these fittings were cast integral to the aluminum barrels.

The M20 and M20B1 had a conical blast deflector on the muzzle, barrel-latch strike and barrel hook on the left side, and a forward-folding bipod. The bipod was adjustable for height by angling the legs forward and locking the slide catch on a notched slide on the barrel's underside. Different styles of bipod slides and catches were found on different launchers. The rear barrel group had a handgrip just behind the forward barrel coupling with a two-finger trigger and a large trigger guard. Early M20s had a single-action safety switch on the upper back of the handgrip – Safe (up), Fire (down). Later M20s and all M20A1s had a double-action safety on the upper left side of the handgrip – Fire (up), Safe (down).

The optical reflecting sight was on the left side and was hinged to fold against the tube. It was provided with a rubber eyepiece and a flip-up protective front cover. The tree-type reticle sight was graduated from 0yd to 400yd at 50yd intervals. The barrel-latch strike and barrel hook, for fastening the two tube sections together, were on the right side. The single-position metal shoulder rest was centered on the rear tube with the height-adjustable telescoping monopod forming part of the forward support for the rest. With the bipod and monopod extended the launcher sat on a form of tripod. It was seldom fired in such a manner, the arrangement mainly used when simply setting it on the ground. A connector coil spring was on both sides of and just forward of the breech. The connector latch was atop the breech and the breech was protected by a conical guard. There was no wire reinforcing on the barrel owing to a much-improved rocket design.

Further improvements were made from lessons learned in combat, resulting in the M20A1 and M20A1B1. New production weapons were not fielded until the final months of the Korean War. However, existing M20s and M20B1s were modified, with the bipod removed and the monopod shoulder rest replaced, and also redesignated M20A1 and M20A1B1. The deletion of the bipod and monopod reduced the launchers' weight by 2lb and 1lb compared to the original M20 and M20B1, respectively. The main difference in the new models was the elimination of the two connector coil springs for attaching the rocket's lead wire and the old connector clamp. These were replaced by a new connector-latch group assembly on top of the breech. This box-like housing had a control handle in the forward end. It

A 3.5in M20A1 rocket launcher, originally an M20 modified to M20A1 standards. It retains the monopod-type rear grip on the shoulder rest, although the internal monopod itself was removed. The optical sight is in the firing position with the front lens cover raised. (Author, courtesy of Texas Military Forces Museum)

THE BAZOOKA EXPOSED

2.36in M1A1 launcher

1. Thin metal tube
2. Contact wire
3. Rear peep sight
4. Metal face guard
5. Wire reinforcing around tube
6. Contact spring
7. M1 sling
8. Battery spring
9. Hinged plate
10. Battery pair
11. Shoulder stock
12. Spare battery pair
13. Circuit indicator light
14. Bar contact
15. Contact switch bar
16. Switch contact
17. Trigger
18. 3-range front sight
19. Mesh muzzle flash deflector

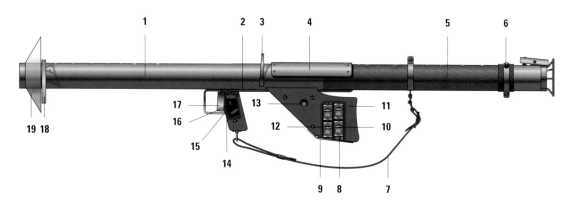

M6A1 HEAT rocket

1. Head
2. Cone
3. Main charge
4. Fuze
5. Motor
6. Tail assembly
7. Fin
8. Igniter wire
9. Nozzle
10. Stabilizer tube
11. Safety pin
12. Body
13. Flange
14. Ogive

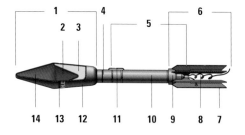

M6A3 HEAT rocket

1. Head
2. Cone
3. Main charge
4. Fuse
5. Safety pin
6. Motor
7. Fins
8. Tail
9. Igniter wire

3.5in M20A1B1 launcher

1. Front barrel assembly
2. Reflecting sight group
3. Rear barrel assembly
4. Cable
5. Contact latch assembly
6. M1 sling
7. Stock
8. Magneto
9. Trigger mechanism
10. Trigger guard
11. Trigger
12. Deflector
13. M20A1B1 combination tool

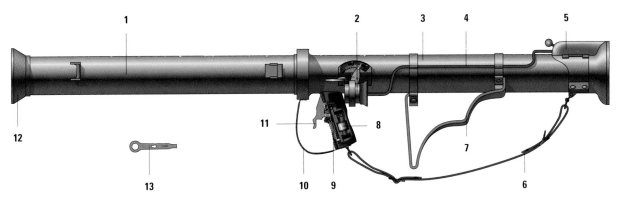

M28A2 HEAT rocket

1. Head
2. Copper cone
3. Main charge
4. Fuse arming pin
5. Fuse
6. Motor
7. Fins
8. Contact ring
9. Groove

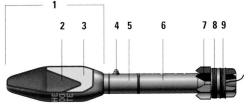

M30 WP rocket

1. Head
2. Steel dome
3. WP smoke charge
4. Burster
5. Fuse arming pin
6. Fuse
7. Motor
8. Contact ring
9. Groove

Experimental bayonet-mounted rocket grenade launcher on M1903 Springfield (1941)

1. Bayonet
2. Grenade launcher
3. Fin (flattened loop)
4. Fin
5. Motor
6. Charge

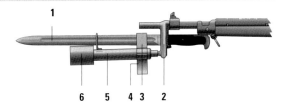

A Texas Army National Guard rifle squad rushes to board its M59 armored personnel carrier (APC) during a Fort Hood, TX, exercise in the early 1960s. Each armored rifle squad of armored divisions had a 3.5in M20A1B1 bazooka aboard its APC without a dedicated crew, but riflemen were trained to use it if needed. The breakdown "three-point-five" was handy when exiting and entering through small vehicle doors, and was convenient for stowing aboard. (Texas Military Forces Museum)

was set down for loading and raised when ready to fire. The latch allowed loading the rocket to a definite stop – making contact when the lever was engaged – and opened the circuit automatically after the rocket was fired. This system eliminated the need to turn the lead wire around a contact post, thus simplifying and speeding up loading by one-third the time. After the Korean War the M20A1B1 became the most common of the bazookas. The 3.5in bazookas were shipped in wooden crates containing four.

There were other little-seen 3.5in rocket launchers. The 3.5in M25 repeating rocket launcher was standardized in 1951, but never issued to units nor was a place found for it in unit organization tables. It was developed in 1950 as the T115E1. The 1948 Conference on Antitank Defense at Fort Monroe, VA, resulted in the 1950 Army Equipment Development Guide, which called for the replacement of the 2.36in M9A1, 3.5in M20, and 57mm M18A1 recoilless rifle by a multipurpose antitank weapon. At this time three 57mm recoilless rifles were assigned to the rifle company's assault section; while being lighter than the M25, and having a much longer range than the standard 3.5in rocket launchers, this weapon had extremely poor armor penetration and bunker-defeating capabilities. The M25 was also much heavier and more awkward than the M20 bazooka, and could only be fired from the M77 tripod. It had little more

3.5in rocket launchers

Model	Weight	Length	Travel length	Effective range	Rate of fire
M20	15lb	60.25in	33in	300yd	4rpm
M20B1	14lb	60.25in	33in	300yd	4rpm
M20A1	13lb	60in	33in	300yd	6rpm
M20A1B1	13lb	60in	33in	300yd	6rpm
M25	100lb	68.5in	39.5in*	350yd	8–10rpm

* Firing mechanism and rear barrel with front barrel section removed.

range than the M20 owing to the M25's barrel being only 8in longer (its forward barrel section was the same as the M20B1's) and it used the same sight. It had a feed hopper on top for three rockets. The bulky feed and firing mechanism made it complex, temperamental, and difficult to maintain. The main disadvantage, however, was that it could not be carried and operated by an individual soldier stalking tanks. It was just another semi-mobile weapon with a significant back-blast signature. It presumably saw limited combat testing in Korea, with 1,500 made.

From 1969 the Navy Riverine Force made limited use of the 3.5in Mk 47 Mod 0 multiple rocket launcher on some 50ft assault support patrol boats (ASPBs). This weapon consisted of four-tube launchers fitted to either side of a Mk 48 Mod 4 turret on the ASPB's forward deck. The turret also mounted two .50cal M2 machine guns. When the machine guns elevated so did the launcher tubes.

Another use of the 3.5in rocket was for the M24 and M66 off-route antitank mines. The M24 underwent a lengthy development by Picatinny Arsenal, NJ, from 1961 until it was adopted in November 1968, when 50,000 were delivered. It comprised a 24in-long plastic M143 launcher tube containing a 3.5in M28A2 HEAT rocket modified with a folding fin assembly and 16yd connecting cable. The cable was attached to an M61 demolition firing device and it in turn to a 24yd wire terminating in a 12yd plastic-covered pressure-activated discriminator switch cable, similar in principle to a service station driveway bell. The launcher was emplaced within 33yd of and perpendicular to a road on which an enemy AFV was expected. It was set up on sandbags, with other sandbags holding it in place, and was aimed to fire into the AFV's hull side or the tracks and road wheels. A throwaway sighting device was provided. The problem was that

The scarcely known 3.5in M25 repeating rocket launcher on its M77 tripod was adopted in 1951, but never issued. The launcher weighed 60lb and the tripod 40lb. Rockets were fed into the hinged, covered top-feed magazine, which held three rounds. It used the same optical sight (on the left side) as used on the M20 rocket launcher, along with the M20's front barrel. (Author, courtesy of Texas Military Forces Museum)

the discriminator cable and wires had to be concealed, unless employed at night. The M66 was similar, but provided with a geophone to detect approaching AFVs through ground vibration. The geophone signaled the data processor, which activated the cross-road infrared beam. Two tripod assemblies, one with an infrared transmitter and the other with a receiver, were hidden on either side of the route and the passing AFV broke the infrared beam to trigger the rocket electrically.

These mines were allocated on the basis of 15 per rifle and engineer company. The M24s' only known combat use was in limited numbers on the Ho Chi Minh Trail in Laos and Cambodia. They were covertly emplaced by Military Assistance Command, Vietnam – Studies and Observations Group (MACV-SOG) reconnaissance teams to interdict North Vietnamese trucks.

2.36in ROCKETS

The launcher was merely a means of delivering the rocket-propelled warhead downrange. The various types of 2.36in rockets consisted of a pressed sheet-metal warhead with a base-detonating fuse at the bottom end, as part of the tailboom. The tailboom contained the propellant charge, bore-riding safety pin, electrical igniter, and fin assembly. Electrical wire leads protruded from the rocket nozzle on the M6A1 and subsequent rockets. All of the various rounds weighed 3.4lb, except for the original M6 (T1) HEAT and M7 (T2) practice, which were 3.5lb. The 2.36in rockets had a muzzle velocity of 265–275fps and maximum range of 700yd. The 2.36in HEAT rockets were packed in individual M87 spiral asphalt-impregnated cardboard tubes with metal end caps. A 128lb wooden case held 20 rounds. There was also a 53lb eight-round box. WP and hexachloroethane (HC) rockets were packed in 68lb wooden boxes with 12 rounds. A total of 15,603,000 2.36in rockets of all types were produced.

Given that the bazooka was primarily an antitank weapon, the HEAT was the most widely used round. HEAT rounds were painted all olive drab with yellow markings. The shaped-charge round was also suitable for attacking bunkers, pillboxes, and other fortified positions constructed of reinforced concrete, masonry, sandbags, and logs and earth. It was also effective against soft-skin vehicles, buildings, and just about anything offering cover. It could be used against exposed troops, but much of the blast effect was directed into the ground and the thin sheet-metal body generated only limited light fragments traveling a moderate distance. Some secondary fragmentation would be created – rocks, gravel, wood pieces, etc. HEAT rounds had very little effect against large obstacles, again because most of the blast was directed into the ground or it made only a small penetrating hole. Multiple rounds would have some destructive effect, but that approach meant expending a considerable amount of ammunition when mortars would be more effective.

A HEAT round detonating against armor plate created a small-diameter hole, slightly larger inside than the entry hole. Besides the molten cone-shaped liner, fragments of the armor, called spalling, were blasted into the

AFV's interior. The same effect occurred when penetrating concrete or masonry. The spalling, though, did not necessarily fill the interior with a shower of deadly fragments. Most traveled down the axis of the penetrating blast. Some could ricochet about the interior. There was blast over-pressure in the interior, but it was seldom disabling.

Practice rounds were identical in size, shape, and weight to their counterpart HEAT rounds to achieve the same trajectory. Inside was a steel rod for weight and a non-functioning fuse, but a live rocket motor. M7 and early-production M7A1 practice rounds were painted all black with white markings. Later M7A1 and subsequent practice models had a light-blue warhead and inert fuse with white markings and an olive-drab tailboom.

The first rocket models for the 2.36in M1 bazooka were the M6 HEAT and M7 practice. These rounds were 21.6in long. The M6 warhead was filled with 0.5lb of pentolite. The M6 had a pointed nose with a contact ring, six long blade-like fins, and a connecting wire taped to the exterior running from the warhead to the fins, and a cord on the safety pin (later models lacked the wire and cord). The M6 rocket's maximum range was 650yd. If the rocket impacted on the ground at ranges under 300yd it usually ricocheted rather than detonated. At ranges over 300yd the angle of impact was steep enough to cause detonation. If impacting in mud, loose sand, deep snow, or water, regardless of range, it often failed to explode.

Misfires were experienced with the M6, requiring an improved igniter squib (a small electric blasting cap-like detonator). More severe

Infantrymen train on the new M9 bazooka, which was issued to combat units in the fall and winter of 1944. This launcher is not loaded; if it were, the tailfins would be seen emerging from the breech. Note the black M87 spiral asphalt-impregnated cardboard packing tubes and rocket arming pins on the ground behind the gunner. (Tom Laemlein/Armor Plate Press)

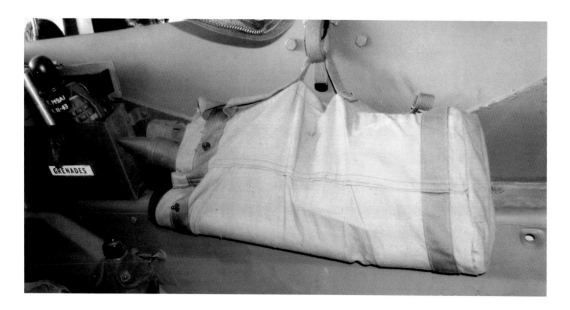

The M6 rocket-carrying bag held three 2.36in rockets, but four could be jammed in. This bag, inside an M20 armored utility car, holds two rockets in tubes: a pointed-nose M6A1 HEAT, and a round-nosed M6A3. The bag is tan with olive-drab reinforcing and carrying straps, but it could be all olive drab. An M9A1 HEAT rifle grenade, which influenced the design of the M6A3 rocket's warhead, can be seen in the box to the left. (Author)

malfunctions also occurred – in-tube motor detonations and failure for all the propellant to burn inside the tube, thus blowing it back on the gunner. Firing of the M6 and M7 rockets was suspended in May 1943 along with the further issue of launchers. This was an Ordnance Department decision made in ignorance of pending operations. Axis forces in North Africa surrendered in May 1943, and the Sicily landing was to launch the following month. An exception was granted for Sicily. Bazookas were not used in the Pacific until December and they were provided with the improved rockets.

The M6A1 HEAT and M7A1 practice rockets were quickly fielded with improved igniter squibs, stabilizer tubes, powder traps, fuse-base covers, and slightly reduced propellant to lessen the chance of premature ignition in low and high temperatures, plus electrical lead wires protruding from the rocket's nozzle were turned around the contact coils near the bazooka's breech. They were the same length as the M6 and M7, but had a 700yd maximum range, as did all later rockets. Ordnance teams were dispatched in July 1943 to modify M1A1 launchers and rockets. M6 rockets modified in-theater by ordnance teams to M6A1 standards were designated M6A2. (Apparently there was no "M7A2" practice round.) Modified M1 launchers as well as M1A1 and M9 launchers could not fire the original M6 and M7 rockets.

In August 1943, the 19.4in-long M6A3 HEAT and M7A3 practice rockets were adopted. They had a round nose to lower the angle of effective impact to 60 degrees, a short cylindrical fin assembly ("barrel fins") with six fins for improved flight stability and to reduce cost, and a waterproof fuse. The main improvement was the replacement of the steel cone-liner with copper to increase penetration by 30 percent, up to 5in. Further developments included the M6A3C, D, and F with different propellants and more sensitive integral fuses to improve detonation with low-angle graze hits. They were further identified by a 0.5in white band on the lower half of the body.

The assistant gunner loads a HEAT rocket into an M9 bazooka in a slit trench. He will have to move well out of the way before the launcher is fired. An M6 rocket carrying bag is in the foreground and needs to be removed from the back-blast area. See Osprey's Fortress 29, *US World War II and Korean War Field Fortifications 1941–53*, for details on bazooka firing positions. (Tom Laemlein/Armor Plate Press)

The final rocket models were developed at the war's end and saw some postwar use. These included the M6A4 and M6A5 HEAT with improved M400 and M401 fuses, respectively, plus other reliability improvements. The practice counterparts were the M7A4 (which replicated the M6A3C and M6A3), M7A5 (which replicated the M6A3D), and M7A6 (which replicated the M6A3F, M6A4, and M6A5) with different propellants. In 1944 the T12 HEAT rocket was tested (T23 practice counterpart) with folding fins, but was never fielded.

M10, and M10A1 through M10A3 WP smoke rockets appeared late in 1944 and were intended for screening, blinding the enemy, and igniting fires. Differences between models were the propellant and fuses. The T27 and T27E1 HC white smoke rounds also appeared in 1944 and, while never standardized, saw limited combat testing. They were intended for marking targets and screening. Upon impact the HC smoke round burned for about one minute. Both WP and HC smoke rockets had light-gray bodies with yellow markings and a yellow band. The tailboom and fuse were olive drab.

A chemical-warfare round was developed and standardized, but was never used in combat. The M26 (T73) was filled with cyanogen chloride (CK), a highly toxic blood agent. It caused immediate effects upon contact with the eyes or lungs: drowsiness, runny nose, sore throat, coughing, confusion, nausea, vomiting, edema, loss of consciousness, convulsions, paralysis, and death within minutes. CK was capable of penetrating gasmask filters. It burst upon impact and in the open the gas dissipated in 10 minutes, but lingered longer in enclosed spaces. The round was light gray with a green band and markings and an olive-drab tailboom and fuse. An incendiary round was also tested, the T12 loaded with thermite. It had a light-gray warhead with a purple band and markings. It was never used in combat.

An antipersonnel rocket was developed for the bazooka in 1943. It was fabricated using two Mk II fragmentation hand grenades attached to a

2.36in rockets and the right bazooka

The wrong HEAT rockets are often shown with incorrect bazooka models in movies, dioramas, and with re-enactors. The M6, M6A1, and M6A2 HEAT rockets had pointed noses and long blade-type fins. The M6 was only fired in the M1 bazooka. The M6A1 and all later models could be fired in the M1A1 and M9 series. Seldom, though, would the pointed nose rockets have been seen with M9-series bazookas. They would be accompanied by the M6A3, A4, and A5, which had a round nose and barrel-type fin assembly. The M10 series WP smoke rockets would only be seen in small numbers from very late 1944.

LEFT A series-production M1 bazooka with the M6 HEAT rocket and the later round-nosed M6A3 HEAT rocket. The M6A1 and later rockets could not be fired in the M1 launcher, nor in M1s modified to M1A1 standards. Nor could the M6 rocket be fired in any later launchers. Existing M6 rockets were modified by ordnance teams to M6A1 standards and redesignated the M6A2. (Hugh Talman, Smithsonian Institution)

bazooka rocket motor. One grenade, with its fuse assembly removed, was attached to the motor by a threaded adapter in the fuse well with the top end down. A double-ended threaded adapter was screwed into the base filler hole of this grenade and a second grenade, with its standard lever-release fuse in place, was screwed into it. A 2.36in-diameter steel disc was placed between the two grenades' bases. The top grenade's arming pin was pulled and the rocket loaded into the launcher with the arming lever riding against the bore. When fired the lever flew off and the grenades burst after the normal 4–5-second delay, allowing an airburst to be achieved. It was little used in combat and never standardized. There were at least two test versions: one using the M6A1 rocket motor with blade fins and the other the M6A3 with barrel-type fins.

3.5in ROCKETS

There were only three types of 3.5in rockets available for the M20 series super bazookas: M28 HEAT, M29 practice, and M30 WP. Rockets were packed in spiral cardboard tubes, three to a 53lb wooden box. The bluntly pointed warheads of all three were the same shape, 23.55in long, and weighed 8.9lb, close to three times that of the 2.36in. Maximum range was 900yd and they had a muzzle velocity of 334fps. They were identified by the same colors as their 2.36in equivalents. The rocket motor was a steel tube containing 12 5in-long sticks of M7 propellant with the M20 igniter in the forward part of the motor and connected to the electrical lead wires protruding from the nozzle. At the upper end of the motor was the M404 base-detonating fuse on the HEAT and WP rounds; the practice round used the M405 inert fuse. The fin assembly consisted of three pairs of fins (six fins in total) within a circular vane. On this was the contact ring to which the connector on the bazooka's breech clamped. This ring was 1.78in wide on the A1 and A2 versions, narrower on the original model.

The M28, M28A1, and M28A2 HEAT warheads were pressed sheet-metal containing 1.93lb of Composition B. (Composition B is a 60/40 mixture of RDX and TNT. It has a relative effect of 1.35 compared to TNT, rated at 1.00.) The M29, M29A1, and M29A2 practice rounds had a sheet-metal windshield with a cast-iron body. They were otherwise empty, with the iron body providing the necessary weight. The T127E2 and M30 (T127E3) smoke rounds' body was filled with 2.33lb of WP topped by a dome-shaped cap. The inside of the pointed windshield was void. Most manuals did not mention the WP rocket, but it did indeed see use.

A 27mm (1.06in) T265 sub-caliber practice rocket was developed for the 3.5in using a launch tube fitted inside the main barrel. It saw scarcely any use as it did not allow for realistic crew drill in rapidly loading the heavy rockets. Another little-used round was the loading-practice round (black with two white bands). It was completely inert and made from earlier test rockets with a different type of four-blade fin.

Two instructors of a 3.5in rocket-launcher training team in August 1950. They provide a comparison of the 3.5in M20 (left) and its M28 HEAT rocket and the 2.36in M9A1 and its M6A3C, D, or F HEAT round, with the more sensitive fuses indicated by the white band on the warhead. (Tom Laemlein/Armor Plate Press)

WARHEAD EFFECTS

The 2.36in M6 HEAT round could penetrate 3in of homogeneous armor at up to a 30-degree angle of impact and 4.7in at zero degrees under ideal conditions. Penetration was increased to 5in at 30 degrees with the M6A3 and later models. This round would also punch through or shatter structural steel such as girders and railroad rails, and penetrate several inches – up to a foot – of masonry, brick, and reinforced concrete, depending on the material's quality. Up to 1ft of timber and 2ft or more of sandbags could be penetrated.

A combat engineer trainee loads a 3.5in M29A2 practice rocket into an M20A1B1 bazooka. Practice rockets had live rocket motors with inert "warheads" weighted the same as the M28A2 HEAT round. The practice round had no marking or smoke charge. It traveled slow enough for the naked eye to see it hit a target tank hulk. (US Army)

The HEAT round's detonation was claimed to be similar to a 75mm howitzer projectile, though with less fragmentation owing to its thin sheet-metal warhead. This claim was an overstatement, as a 75mm projectile contained 1.47lb of TNT compared to the bazooka's 0.5lb of pentolite. (Pentolite is a 50/50 mixture of PETN and TNT with a relative effect of 1.26 compared to TNT's rating of 1.00.) The fragmentation effect was slightly greater than the 60mm mortar HE, however.

The 3.5in HEAT round could penetrate up to 11in of armor and was able to defeat any contemporary tank. In an antipersonnel role it threw a 10yd-wide, 20yd-deep fragmentation pattern. The HEAT round could penetrate at least 2ft of masonry, reinforced concrete, and timbers plus at least 3ft of sandbags.

There were complaints of 2.36in and sometimes 3.5in rockets bouncing off enemy tanks and they were accused of not being able to penetrate the armor. That had nothing to do with the ability of the round to penetrate or the thickness of the armor – it was because the warhead struck at such a steep angle that the shaped charge failed to detonate and the projectile glanced off. Most soldiers at the time did not fully understand the mechanics of how the shaped-charge projectile worked. They naturally equated it to conventional armor-piercing rounds and how they were defeated by thick armor. The projectile lacked a graze capability allowing it to detonate if striking at a steeper angle. This glancing off occurs to varying degrees with most HEAT rockets, recoilless weapons, and rifle grenades.

The 2.36in M10 series WP rounds were of the bursting type (0.28oz EC blank fire powder) that created a dense cloud of screening smoke and threw WP particles burning at 5,000°F to a distance of 10–15yd from the impact point. These rounds were effective against bunkers and open-topped fighting positions, showering flaming WP into the positions. WP particles burn through flesh to the bone, will smear when wiped, and cannot be extinguished except by smothering with mud, petroleum jelly, etc. The 3.5in M29 series WP round with the M8 bursting charge also scattered WP 10–15yd from the impact point.

USE
The tank-killer in action

Regardless of the surprisingly accurate hits on a moving tank achieved during the bazooka's debut, its development was rushed and the weapon had not endured the usual rigorous engineering processes and proving ground trials, so it was far from perfect. Only the test of battle would verify whether it was a viable weapon.

Gen Marshall's rush order of 5,000 bazookas in May 1942 was destined for the hard-pressed British and Soviets. The British at Suez received 600 M1 bazookas in September 1942. The M1s were field tested and deemed to be unsuited for desert warfare. It was reasoned that infantrymen could not approach within the 200yd range of German armor due to the lack of concealment in the desert. This was a reasonable assessment in that tanks operated in groups and were accompanied by infantry. Apparently not considered was the bazooka's value as a defensive weapon when a position was attacked by tanks. The British shipment was simply placed in storage. Britain later received another 1,500, but they may have been delivered to the French Resistance.

On the other hand, the Soviets employed their allotted 3,000 M1 bazookas, although they were not overly impressed. (Some sources say the Soviets received 8,500 bazookas, but that was the number of HEAT rounds.) They conducted field testing and concluded that the bazooka's effective armor penetration was just 2–2.2in; that it had low accuracy beyond 50–100yd; was difficult to fire from a dug-in position owing to back-blast, and difficult to conceal because of the smoke and dust signature. In addition, there was a danger of hand injuries to crewmen as well as a threat to nearby personnel owing to unburnt propellant and the unpredictability of the rocket's flight in cold weather. The Soviets therefore opted to stay with the heavier and awkward 14.5mm antitank rifle. Regardless, the Soviet used some bazookas in combat and these, not bazookas in American hands in Tunisia, were the first to be captured to

An American soldier points out the details and explains the operation of an M1 bazooka to British officers. The M1 lacked sling attachments, and here a rope has been fastened as a makeshift sling. This M1 lacks the forward handgrip. (Tom Laemlein/Armor Plate Press)

provide the impetus for the German 8.8cm *Panzerschreck*. Their finding of the 2in-plus armor penetration may be the difference between optimistic US testing against vertical armor and the Soviets' more pessimistic testing against sloped armor. In spite of the Soviets' dismal assessment, they went on to develop the successful RPG-2 and RPG-7 antitank weapons.

Lend-Lease bazookas

Country	Launchers	HEAT	Practice
Britain	2,127*	86,000	1,630
Brazil	2,876	1,000†	2,000
Canada	171	49,220	85
China	2,018	376,900	1,000
French *maquis*	2,616	?	0
Free French	11,350	0†	0
USSR	3,000	8,500	1,605

* The British bazookas may have been among those supplied to the French *maquis* and Yugoslavian partisans via the Special Operations Executive (SOE).

† Additional rockets issued through US supply channels.

BAZOOKAS IN THE MEDITERRANEAN THEATER

Units in the States began training on the bazooka in December 1942, but units overseas did not initially have this benefit. The first US combat use of the M1 bazooka was on November 8, 1942 during Operation *Torch*, just four months after it was formally adopted. Operation *Torch* launched six US divisions and British forces, sailing from the United States and Britain, to land in French Morocco and Algeria. The Vichy French armor threat was minimal (210 obsolescent tanks) and German and Italian armored forces were far to the east facing Commonwealth forces in Egypt. The invasion force had been hastily assembled and loaded. Among the masses of equipment, materiel, and supplies loaded were crates marked "Launcher, rocket, antitank, 2.36-in, M1," each holding six of the new weapons. There were no manuals, no training teams, no one with any knowledge of what they even were. Officers inspecting the cargo aboard some ships found the words "antitank" in particular catching their attention. They also discovered crates of rockets. Some adventurous officers broke out the weapons and after experimentation figured out how to load and fire the weapons. They did some test-firing off the fantail and then began training the troops. There were not many rockets available, so many of the rocket gunners who would be carrying them into combat had only seen demonstration firings. Not all units came ashore armed with bazookas and none knew they was so nicknamed.

One of the first engagements involving a bazooka – details are lacking – occurred when a lone soldier bearing a bazooka separated himself from his unit and approached a Vichy coastal defense fortress armed with 155mm guns. He fired a single rocket at the rear entrance and the fortress commander surrendered. Another unit moving inland detected six Vichy tanks in an attack position. A rocket was fired into their midst to strike a tree. The Vichy commander thought they were under artillery fire and again surrendered. The bazookas were used to good effect defending roadblocks. In one instance, a lieutenant moved up and down a seawall firing from multiple positions to make the Vichy believe they were under fire by a 75mm howitzer battery. Through the rest of the North Africa campaign bazookas saw only limited use. It may be possible that they killed no tanks.

Some units did not receive bazookas until February when they were in Tunisia, and soon began to use them to engage the *Deutsches Afrikakorps*. The US soldiers were yet to receive manuals, and they had to experiment through trial and error on how to use them. The lack of manuals meant there were no prescribed tactics either, not that the manuals would have been of much

An 83rd Infantry Division soldier in Belgium displays an M1A1 bazooka, January 1945. Note the Eveready 791-A battery attached to the shoulder stock by tacked tin C-ration can stripes and held in place by tape over the top end. There is a spare battery inside the stock, but batteries lasted only briefly in cold weather, so it appears he has made arrangements for an additional spare. Besides the bazooka he is armed with an M1 rifle and an M1 carbine. (Tom Laemlein/Armor Plate Press)

help. The early manuals covered description, functioning, operation, malfunctions and corrections, care, disassembly and assembly, inspection, maintenance, and other administrative and technical aspects. They offered little in the way of tactical advice, simply because the bazooka's rushed fielding did not allow the Infantry School to test concepts and integrate them into unit tests and exercises. Units in combat had to learn how to use them in the face of the enemy.

The early tactics, if they could be called that, were simplistic and failed to provide techniques for multiple bazooka engagements and mutual support. The tendency was for individual bazooka teams to engage tanks from defensive positions or to stalk them using cover and concealment. Seldom were two or three teams positioned covering an avenue of approach or sector for mutually supporting fire, i.e., the teams all covering the same sector from different positions, allowing the target to be attacked from different directions and ranges. That way, if one or more weapons were knocked out or forced to withdraw, the sector was still covered by at least one other weapon.

Patton's Third Army viewed bazookas as a last-resort weapon to be employed when infantry were being overrun by tanks. As far as they were concerned, it was not intended to hunt tanks offensively. Recognizing that bazookas revealed a soldier's position when fired and that they were none too accurate at longer ranges, Third Army instructions specified that men were to hold their fire until at 30yd range. It was thought if the bazooka team remained concealed and held its fire until certain of a killing hit, it would not be detected by accompanying enemy infantry and avoid the tank's machine guns. Of course, this approach was not possible in many situations and bazooka men had to engage the enemy as they saw fit.

The Ordnance Department strove to make the M1A1 and improved rockets available for the June 1943 invasion of Sicily, but it was not to be.

An armorer cleans M9 bazookas aboard a ship off Okinawa. It was easier to swab out the tubes when they were broken down into two sections. Being painted and with few moving parts, bazookas were simple to maintain. The bore was kept lightly oiled and the trigger mechanism and rocket connector latch were lubricated. (Tom Laemlein/Armor Plate Press)

Members of the 17th Airborne Division warm up in January 1945 in Douzy, France. Airborne units were among the first to receive the M9 and thus their weapons often had the simple bar sight rather than the optical reflex sight. (Tom Laemlein/Armor Plate Press)

The further issue and use of bazookas and rockets had been restricted on the eve of Operation *Husky*. However, an exception was granted and M1 bazookas saw wide and successful use during the six-week operation.

Bazookas were considered critical for the Sicily operation as counterattacks were expected by Panzer Division *Hermann Göring*. The paratroopers of the 82nd Airborne Division were especially keen on the bazooka. These men were to be dropped in small groups beyond the beachhead to interdict counterattacks, and would be the first to engage the Panzers. Each platoon formed a two-man bazooka team. The July 9, 1943, jump was scattered, with paratroopers distributed all over the countryside. The bazooka-armed roadblocks and roving groups led the Germans to believe there were more paratroopers than there actually were. Col James Gavin, commanding the 505th Parachute Infantry Regiment, contracted nuns at a convent to hand-sew bazooka patches after the campaign. The patches were presented to bazooka gunners who had knocked out tanks. The real value of the bazooka was discovered on Sicily, as it was used extensively to knock out field fortifications. It would be recognized as being as valuable in this role as it was as a tank-killer

By the beginning of the campaign on the Italian mainland in September 1943, the bazooka was fully accepted and its value realized. The M1A1 was now available, as well as M1s modified to M1A1 standards. It proved valuable for attacking tanks, with teams maneuvering through the mountainous terrain and town rubble to get within striking distance. It was widely used for attacking bunkers, fortifications, and troops hidden in ravines. The bazooka's value was enhanced by its light weight, making it easy to haul across the steep, rugged ground. Mortars and their ammunition were heavy and bulky, but were still valuable, as their high-angle trajectory could reach behind ridges and into ravines. Bazookas, though, could be easily carried into position to deliver direct fire on hard-to-get-at targets, even if only at short range.

One example of the use of the M1A1 bazooka was in May 1944 near Carano, Italy. Tech Sgt Van Barfoot, a platoon sergeant in the 157th Infantry, 45th Infantry Division, found his platoon bogged down in an assault against a well-dug-in enemy on high ground. Barfoot struck off alone and attacked a machine-gun emplacement with a hand grenade, killing two Germans and wounding three. Working his way to another machine-gun nest, he Tommy-gunned two enemy and captured three. Seeing this performance, another machine-gun crew surrendered without resistance. Leaving the prisoners for one of his following squads, he rounded up more prisoners, totaling 17. After reorganizing his platoon and consolidating the ground he gained, he prepared for a counterattack. This arrived in the form of three PzKpfw V Panther tanks. Arming himself with an M1A1 bazooka and completely exposing himself ahead of the rolling tanks, Barfoot knocked the track off the lead tank at 75yd. The other two withdrew to the flank to avoid him and with his Thompson he killed three crewmen abandoning the disabled tank. Barfoot advanced into enemy-held ground and destroyed an abandoned artillery piece with a demolition charge. He returned to his platoon and assisted critically wounded men to a distant aid station. His aggressive action under direct enemy fire inspired his platoon to continue the advance and resulted in his being awarded the Medal of Honor.

FIRING THE 2.36in M1 SERIES BAZOOKAS

One of the bazooka's better attributes is that it was simple to operate, and therefore easy and quick to train crews to use the weapon. There were several safety considerations that had to be observed, and which applied to the M9 series as well the 3.5in versions:

1. The propellant burned in 0.02–0.03 seconds and combustion was complete before the rocket left the tube. If the combustion was retarded in even the least amount it could create a back-flash when the rocket left the muzzle. This could occur in cold weather (see below) and it was recommended that the operator wear gloves and eye protection. A "rocket launcher face mask" was issued. It consisted of a pair of goggles with a rubber-coated cloth face guard. Gasmasks were sometimes used. In lieu of gloves it was recommended wrapping cloth around the hands. The wearing of steel helmets was also recommended. In combat gloves and face protection were seldom worn, though they were sometimes in the winter.

2. The bazooka could be fired from standing, kneeling, sitting, or prone positions. From the prone position the firer's legs had to be angled at 45 degrees to the direction of fire to avoid back-blast injury.

2.36in M9A1 ROCKET LAUNCHER CREW DRILL

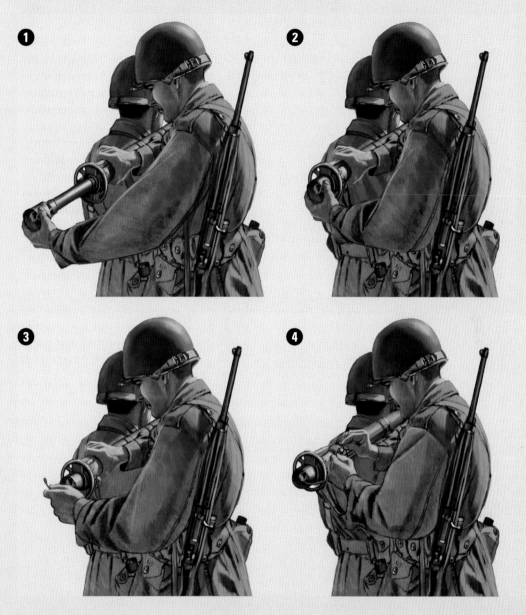

The launcher is shown being loaded from the right side, but it could be loaded from the left side just as easily. This depended on whether the loader was right- or left-handed and the available cover and concealment. Prior to loading the M9A1 gunner ensures the safety lever is on "Safe." With the earlier M1A1 the gunner first tested the circuit by squeezing the trigger several times. The indicator light should light only when the trigger is squeezed. The gunner ensures the light is out and that he is not squeezing the trigger. The M9A1 loader then: (**1**) inserts the rocket warhead partially into the breech and removes the arming pin; (**2**) raises the tail latch atop the breech and pushes the rocket fully into the launcher, ensuring the latch locks the rocket in place; (**3**) removes the coiled contact wire from the inside of the fin assembly, stretching it out; (**4**) wraps the uninsulated end of the wire around the contact spring (one on either side of the tube). Once the launcher is loaded the loader taps the gunner and calls, "Up!" letting him know that the loader has checked to the rear and it is clear of personnel and obstructions and the launcher is ready to fire. The gunner then aims and engages the target. The loading procedure for the M1 and M1A1 bazookas was virtually identical to the M9A1 loading sequence shown here.

3. It was essential that no personnel, equipment, or flammable materials be within a cone-shaped area 20ft deep and 20ft wide behind the bazooka. The back-blast was quite powerful and would kill a man in the area. Nor could there be obstructions to the rear that would reflect back-blast onto the crew. These obstructions included rear parapets of fighting positions, walls, and trees. If the bazooka was elevated too high, the back-blast could reflect off the ground or other objects.

4. The bazooka could only be fired within buildings from large rooms with sufficient rear clearance and at least an open door or large window. Even in good conditions, the overpressure could still be uncomfortable, hurting the ears.

5. The rockets could not be fired in temperatures below 0°F and above 120°F, as the propellant would only partially ignite resulting in muzzle back-flash and erratic performance, or failure to ignite at all. This could occasionally occur at temperatures between 0°F and 70°F too, although the effects were less serious.

6. The loader had to ensure he stayed clear of the breech and danger area at all times. He never stood behind the launcher.

To load the bazooka, the gunner placed the launcher on his right shoulder, aiming it down-range. He first tested the circuit by squeezing the trigger several times. The indicator light on the stock should have lit only when the trigger was pressed. The gunner had to ensure the light was out and kept his fingers off the trigger while the rocket was loaded. On the M1, the loader ensured the connector box's arming lever was in the down (Safe) position. He raised the tail latch, inserted just the warhead into the breech, closed the tail latch, removed the arming pin from the rocket, raised the tail latch, pushed the rocket fully in, and lowered the tail latch to engage in notches on the fins.

On the M1A1, which had no connector box, the loader raised the tail latch, inserted the warhead into the breech, closed the tail latch, removed the arming pin from the rocket, raised the tail latch, pushed the rocket fully in, and lowered the tail latch to engage in notches on the fins.

He then pulled the lead wire straight back out of the rocket nozzle, uncoiling it and wrapping it around either of the coiled spring contacts just forward of the breech. Once loaded the safety was set to "Fire."

With both the M1 and M1A1, the gunner estimated the range and chose the appropriate stud on the front sight, aligning it with the target and peep sight. The gunner squeezed and released the trigger, which ignited the rocket motor. The propellant ignited in a loud crack with blast and a quick flash out the breech. There was virtually no muzzle flash or smoke. The gunner experienced absolutely no recoil – the sudden absence of 3.4lb from the shoulder was noticed, but no recoil was felt.

To unload the launcher, the loader unwound the lead wire from the contact spring, raised the tail latch, and withdrew the rocket. He then reinserted the arming pin, coiled and placed the wire between the fins, and returned the rocket to a packing tube.

CREWING AND ALLOCATION OF 2.36in BAZOOKAS

When bazookas were allocated to units and added to their Tables of Organization and Equipment (TO&E) in 1942–43, there were no dedicated crews. The firer might have been called a rocket gunner or operator, bazooka-man, or rocketeer. Army rifle companies were authorized three bazookas in March 1943, even though some units received them earlier. These were assigned to the weapons platoon headquarters and typically allotted one to each rifle platoon. There might be a couple of men in each squad trained to operate the bazooka or a two-man dedicated crew designated in each platoon. Five additional bazookas were authorized for rifle companies in February 1944. Now each rifle company had a total of eight bazookas, and an additional dedicated crew might be assigned in each platoon and other launchers kept as spares.

Parachute rifle companies were first assigned four bazookas, to be issued as necessary. From February 1944 they were allocated one per platoon headquarters and one in the company headquarters. Often four two-man bazooka crews were formed under company control, to be detailed to platoons as needed. Glider rifle companies had a pool of five or six bazookas allotted as necessary. (Until early 1945 glider companies had only two platoons.) Ranger platoons had one bazooka with a dedicated crew. The 1st Special Service Force had two bazookas per platoon. Armored rifle platoons had five halftracks divided between the platoon headquarters (which contained its own rifle squad), two rifle squads, a machine-gun squad, and a mortar squad. Each squad possessed a trained crew to man their bazooka as needed.

From the beginning of 1948, rifle platoons received a weapons squad with a machine gun and bazooka. This was the first time the Army had formally assigned dedicated bazooka crews – rocket gunner, assistant gunner, and two ammunition bearers. It was with this organization that the Army entered the Korean War.

The Marine Corps did not assign bazookas to unit TO&E until 1943, and then on the basis of three in rifle company headquarters. As with the Army, the Marines did not initially provide dedicated crews, although most units detailed crews out of rifle platoons. It was not uncommon for additional bazookas to be loaned from battalion. In combat, companies often task-organized assault squads with bazookas and flamethrowers. On Iwo Jima in February 1945, provisional assault platoons were formed by each battalion. This structure was formalized and incorporated into battalion TO&E by the time of the April 1945 Okinawa landing. The Marine infantry battalion therefore had a dedicated assault platoon organized into three sections, each with two seven-man squads: each of these squads included a squad leader, two-man bazooka team, two-man flamethrower team, and two demolitions men. The Marines retained the battalion assault platoon after World War II, eventually assigning 18 bazookas.

The M6 rocket-carrying bag was issued on the basis of two per bazooka (three per bazooka in infantry companies). The canvas bag held three rockets and could be carried by an adjustable shoulder strap or

A paratrooper of the 101st Airborne Division boards a C-47 transport for a pre-invasion practice jump in Britain in 1943. The 54.5in-long M1A1 was awkward for paratroopers to jump with. It was less than desirable to drop the launchers in separate containers, where they might not be found. The sling was secured beneath the parachute harness, and padded canvas muzzle and breech covers fitted. The Airborne Command requested a takedown bazooka, resulting in the M9 in late 1944. (Getty Images)

carrying handle. The parachutist's model had a "V" ring and snap hook on the back, allowing it to be attached to the harness, and tie-tapes on the bottom to secure it to the leg. The M2 ammunition bag, a carrying vest for 60mm and 81mm mortar rounds, was used as a substitute carrier. Its large front and back pockets each held four rockets.

BAZOOKAS IN THE EUROPEAN THEATER

The June 1944 Normandy landings saw the M1A1 bazooka widely issued to all US units, and it remained the primary bazooka through 1944. Airborne units were the first to receive M9s; the 1st Airborne Task Force air-assaulting into southern France in August 1944 was equipped with the M9, the earliest date of its use. They began to be issued to other units in August–October and were in wide distribution by January 1945. The M9 was mainly issued to infantry, reconnaissance, and other combat units, however, while headquarters, service, and support units retained the M1A1, many to the war's end.

An assault team of the 2nd Ranger Infantry Battalion aboard a British landing craft, assault (LCA) in Weymouth Harbour on June 5, 1944, prepared to depart for Pointe-du-Hoc, Normandy. The bazookaman holds a 2.36in M1A1 rocket launcher providing a good view of the mesh flash deflector. To the left is an M1 bangalore torpedo lashed to an M1 rifle. (Hulton Archive/Getty)

A staged scene, but supposedly re-enacted by the bazooka crew that actually killed this Panther tank in Normandy. There is already a rocket loaded in the tube and the loader is insufficiently clear of the back-blast danger area. (© Hulton-Deutsch Collection/Corbis)

While the Germans were incapable of mounting *Blitzkrieg*-scale operations – with the exception of the December 1944 Ardennes Offensive (the Battle of the Bulge) – they were still able to mount local offensive actions and counterattacks with meaningful numbers of tanks and assault guns. US antitank capabilities were therefore necessary at all echelons. Large numbers of tank destroyer and separate tank battalions were available, along with 57mm and 3in antitank guns. The bazooka remained important as a unit antitank self-defense weapon. They were immensely valuable to the infantry, not only as tank killers, but for defeating fortified buildings, field fortifications, and *Westwall* (Siegfried Line) bunkers, and they served well as a close-support weapon.

From D-Day in Normandy to the end of the war, all US units arriving in Europe had conducted ample training on the bazooka. It was no longer the mysterious weapon discovered in the cargo hold while en route to a hostile beachhead. The following are extreme examples of valor, man-against-tank duels in which the subject soldiers were awarded the Medal of Honor. For those with the individual willingness to close with the enemy at short ranges, often fully exposed, the lightweight bazooka gave them the tool to outmaneuver and stalk enemy tanks.

Staff Sgt Clyde Choate of the 601st Tank Destroyer Battalion demonstrated stalking a tank with an M1A1 bazooka in October 1944 outside Bruyères, France. Sgt Choate's lone M10 tank destroyer was positioned to support a rifle company defending a small hill. A German company attacked at dusk with a single PzKpfw IV tank in support. The Panzer scored two hits on the M10 and Choate ordered his crew out of the burning vehicle. After reaching safety, Choate could not account for all his men, so returned to the burning M10 and found none of the crew left behind. The enemy fire was intense – his jacket was holed and his helmet knocked off by the rounds. He recovered a bazooka when he saw that the German infantry and tank were overrunning the American company's foxholes. Darting from tree to tree, he made his way through enemy skirmishers and got to within 20yd of the PzKpfw IV. He halted it by knocking off a track, but the tank was still able to fire its main gun and machine guns. Braving rifle and machine-gun fire, Choate dashed back to the M10 and found another rocket. He again made his way under fire to within 10yd of the Panzer and this time placed a shot on the side of its turret. He killed two crewmen with his pistol and then mounted the tank under fire and threw grenades inside. Seeing their lone supporting tank in flames, the German infantry wavered and the American riflemen counterattacked, driving the Germans away from a US battalion command post behind the American position.

Pfc Carl Sheridan was a bazooka gunner with the 47th Infantry, 9th Infantry Division, participating in an attack on Frezenberg Castle near Weisweiler, Germany, in November 1944. After assaulting across 1,000yd of open ground under artillery and mortar fire, his unit gained a foothold in two buildings. Sheridan's loader was wounded during the rush, but Sheridan recovered a rocket bag. Some 70 German paratroopers were defending the castle's massive stone gatehouse. The castle was surrounded by a 20ft-deep moat and Sheridan saw that the only way to enter the strongpoint was over a drawbridge through a barricaded stout wooden gate. Understanding he had the only weapon capable of breaching the gate, he rushed into the open courtyard under a hail of small-arms fire and grenades. Taking up a completely exposed position at the end of the drawbridge, he fired two rounds into the gate, damaging but not breaching it. Loading his last rocket he took careful aim and breached the oaken gate. Shouting, "Come on, let's get them!" he charged through the gate firing his .45cal pistol. Pfc Sheridan died in the heavy fire, but led the way for the rest of his company to storm the strongpoint.

Metz area, October 1944. An ad hoc 90th Infantry Division assault team armed with an M1A1 bazooka and an M1918A2 BAR with the bipod removed, a common practice. The loader holds an M6A1 HEAT rocket. Sling attachment swivels were fitted on the M1A1 and later bazookas. (Tom Laemlein/Armor Plate Press)

In December 1944, Pfc William Soderman of the 9th Infantry, 2nd Infantry Division, armed with an M9 bazooka, was manning a roadblock with his loader near Rocherath, Belgium. A heavy artillery barrage wounded his loader and Soderman sent him to the rear. Five PzKpfw VI Tiger tanks were driving down the road in the dusk. Soderman stood in full view of the massive tanks at point-blank range and knocked out the first one with a single shot. The crew abandoned the burning Tiger and the others passed by before he could reload. He remained at the roadblock all night under heavy artillery, mortar, and machine-gun fire. Soon after dawn, five more tanks (type not specified) approached. He rushed through a ditch to position himself near the tanks. Repeating his previous performance, he leapt into the road directly in front of the tanks and knocked out the leader. Unable to pass the burning tank and halted by deep roadside ditches, the other tanks withdrew. Soderman fell back to his position, but encountered a German platoon. Firing another rocket, he killed at least two soldiers and wounded several others. His company was ordered to withdraw to an assembly area owing to flanking attacks. Soderman heard tanks approaching the position and, realizing some company elements were still engaged, rushed forward, and again destroyed a lead tank with a single bazooka shot. Withdrawing, he was hit in the shoulder and crawled through a ditch to an American position, from which he was evacuated.

Pfc George Turner of the 499th Armored Field Artillery Battalion, 14th Armored Division, was caught separated from his unit by a Panzergrenadier attack in Philippsbourg, France, in January 1945. Turner linked up with a withdrawing armored rifle company and observed two PzKpfw IV tanks and about 75 grenadiers advancing down the village's main street. He found an M9 bazooka and worked his way down the street under small-arms and tank fire. Standing exposed in the middle of

Infantrymen preceded by a 3in gun-armed M10 tank destroyer wearily make their way through a French village during the drive to Paris in August 1944. There were no dedicated rocket gunners in rifle platoons. Either individuals were trained as an additional duty or in some cases a two-man team was formed in each platoon. This gunner carries an M1A1 with its wire-mesh muzzle-flash protector still attached. It was common for these to be knocked off or intentionally removed. (Tom Laemlein/Armor Plate Press)

HEADQUARTERS
5th TANK DESTROYER GROUP
APO 758, U.S. ARMY

1. To ascertain from first hand observation the effect of bazooka fire on the Mk V Panther tank, 16 rounds were fired at a knocked out 130 Pz. Lehr [Division] Mk V, which had been immobilized by the 776th TD Bn's 90mm fire (M36).

2. Diagram of tank indicating location of hits:

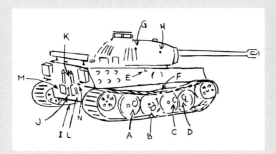

DESCRIPTION OF HITS

a. Ricochet into wheel rim completely severing the tire and blasting an 8" hole in the wheel. There was no damaging effect upon the inner wheel immediately behind the one hit.

b. Direct hit upon a wheel. A 3×5" hole was blasted out of the wheel and two 10" radial cracks were made. There was no damaging effect upon the wheel immediately inside the one hit.

c. & d. Direct hits upon wheels. 6" diameter holes blasted – no effect upon inner wheels.

e. Hit scored one inch below upper edges of side skirt. While the deck plating served to add thickness at the point of contact, a complete penetration was made, the hole being of sufficient diameter at this smallest point to allow an ordinary pencil to pass completely into the interior.

f. A hit upon the bolt holding two adjacent track plates together. The head of the bolt was sheared away completely, though the track plates were not damaged. It is possible that the bolt could have worked out, thus severing the track.

g. A hit upon the corner of the turret, making a complete penetration. The hole was cylindrical, ¾" in diameter, with little flaking or enlargement on the inner surface. The blast effect was evident on the inside by the particles of steel having ricocheted from one side to the other.

h. A turret hit making a similar ¾" hole with flaking on the inner surface of about 4" in diameter around the hole. There were approximately 36 small craters on the inner surface of the opposite turret armor, each at least ⅛" deep and from ⅛"–⅜" in diameter. As the face of each pit was smooth, the blast effect of the flying particles must be terrific. The area covered by these craters was roughly 8"–10" in diameter.

i. A hit upon the very bottom edge of the rear plate. The projectile just grazed the armor and only a small nick was chipped out of the armor. The projectile did detonate, but the effect was underneath the tank in the ground.

j. A hit upon the towing-jack device on the rear of the tank. A small portion was chipped away, but there was no effect upon the armor plate.

k. A hit upon one of the exhaust pipes, completely blasting it away, but there was no effect upon the armor plate inasmuch as the blast had been dissipated upon the exhaust pipe.

l. A ricochet off the rear armor, detonating in the ground.

m. & n. Two hits in the rear armor, each making a clean penetration, the hole being ½" in diameter through armor plate 2" thick.

o. A hit upon the lower portion of the front armor plate. No penetration was made. A 1½" long gash, ½" deep, and ¼" wide was gouged away.

p. A hit upon the towing hook on the front of the tank. No damaging effect upon the armor plate.

3. CONCLUSIONS:

The bazooka will penetrate the armor on the side, rear, and side of the turret on the German Mk. V Panther tank. The turret is very effectively penetrated and the blasted particles on the inside most certainly are lethal. The side armor is of less thickness than the turret and can be penetrated more easily.

The wheel and tracks are not profitable targets. Pieces may be blown out of the wheel or tires cut, but the possibility of stopping the tank is remote.

The rear armor is a profitable target, because the engine compartment is very susceptible to fire, even though the tool boxes, jacks and exhausts are reduce the area of vulnerability.

Upon the front armor, it is difficult to get an effective burst, as the slope of the armor will ricochet the rocket. No perpendicular hits were obtained during the trial.

For the Group Commander:

EDWARD N. STIVER
Major, F.A.
S-2

the street, he knocked out the lead tank, reloaded, and damaged the second, halting it. He rushed to an abandoned US M3 halftrack, dismounted its .30cal machine gun, and set it up in the street to take the German infantry under fire. Killing and wounding a large number, he forced their withdrawal. US troops counterattacked after he halted the tanks, but two M4 Sherman tanks were knocked out by an antitank gun. Turner provided suppressing fire from the machine gun, firing from the hip, so the halted US tank crews could escape. One wounded man was unable to extract himself and Turner ran under fire to the tank to aid him. The tank's ammunition detonated, seriously wounding Turner. Refusing evacuation, he remained with the infantry through the next day to help drive off an attack, aid in the capture of a strongpoint, and drive a truck through enemy fire transporting wounded to an aid station.

AIRBORNE AND NAVAL BAZOOKAS

BELOW

Airborne bazookas. Maj Charles "Bazooka Charlie" Carpenter connects a rocket's lead wire to the contact post on modified M1A1 bazookas fitted to the wing struts of his L-4H spotter aircraft. The shoulder stock and handgrip were removed and a solenoid trigger system installed. This was an early mounting with two launchers under each wing. He later mounted three under each wing. (US Army)

BELOW RIGHT

The business end of the Navy's Mk 1 sextuple rocket launcher, mounting six modified M1A1 bazookas. Note the Plexiglas blast shield and the use of goggles. Only one launcher retained its sights. (US Navy)

Lightweight compact bazookas and the imagination of American fighting men led to unusual uses. There were a number of instances in which bazookas were mounted under-wing on Piper L-4 and Stinson/Consolidated L-5 aircraft, two-seat planes used for scouting and artillery spotting. Two or three 2.36in M1A1 bazookas were sometimes jury-rigged under each wing and fired with solenoid triggers. They were used to mark targets and in a few cases to attack enemy armor, but were of only marginal success owing to the bazooka's short accurate range. They were better suited for target marking and harassment.

One example of airborne bazooka applications was Maj Charles "Bazooka Charlie" Carpenter, also known as "The Mad Major" and "Lucky Carpenter." Assigned to the 4th Armored Division in France, he fitted three bazookas under each wing of his L-4H "Rosie the Rocketeer." Unilaterally he attacked German tank formations, with some success. Carpenter was on the verge of being court-martialed for unauthorized modifications and risk-taking, but Patton intervened and instead decorated "Lucky Carpenter," citing him as an example of his principle of "attack, attack and then attack again." "Bazooka Charlie" was credited with killing six tanks and was presented the Silver Star and an Air Medal. "The Mad

Major" was also known to land his plane when he saw a ground action and lend a hand.

A more down-to-earth use of the bazooka, but still not ground-bound, was its use aboard patrol torpedo boats (PTs) and motor gunboats (PGMs) in the southwest Pacific. In late 1943 the Navy developed the 2.36in Mk 1 sextuple rocket launcher, a modified Mk 19 .30cal machine-gun pedestal mount with six modified M1A1 bazookas. These were mounted atop the day cabin aft of the cockpit and pilot house on a small number of boats. Expedient two- and four-tube versions were also used. The main drawback of this setup was again the bazooka's short range, making the multiple rocket launcher less than ideal for attacking Japanese supply barges. They were typically able to obtain at least two hits out of a six-rocket ripple salvo at 250yd. Rockets often failed to detonate if hitting wooden targets or when striking the water, but could be skip-fired into watercraft hulls. There were instances of Army units mounting similar dual-tube M1A1 launchers on jeeps.

Some reconnaissance units mounted jury-rigged M1A1 bazookas on M31 machine-gun pedestal mounts aboard ¼-ton scout jeeps. The left launcher is a production M1A1 while the right is a former M1 modified to M1A1 standards, but still with the forward handgrip. (US Army)

FIRING THE 2.36in M9 SERIES BAZOOKAS

The M9 series and M18 operated very much like the M1A1. If the launcher was in the travel mode, the two barrel sections were separated by releasing the barrel latch behind the handgrip and pivoting the front barrel away from the rear section when the barrel-latch strike was released. The front barrel's hook was disengaged from the rear barrel's hook eye.

The front barrel's coupling screw (on its rear end) was inserted into the coupling nut on the forward end of the rear barrel, engaging the interrupted screw thread. The front barrel was rotated 60 degrees clockwise, the coupling lock lever clicked, and the barrel was locked in place. To unlock the barrel sections the coupling lock lever was depressed and the front barrel rotated 60 degrees counterclockwise and the two sections separated.

The gunner aimed the launcher down-range, ensured the safety was on "Safe" (up), and kept his fingers off the trigger. The launcher was loaded in the same manner as the M1A1. With the folding bar sight the gunner estimated the range and set the range indicator pointer on the appropriate range marker and aligned the front sight stud and peep sight with the target. The gunner moved the safety lever to "Fire" (down) and squeezed and released the trigger, igniting the rocket motor. The 6.5in-longer barrel further reduced the chance of muzzle flash and blow-back. Unloading was the same as the M1A1, except that the weapon was placed on "Safe."

53

BAZOOKAS IN THE PACIFIC THEATER

Bazookas arrived in the Pacific a year after their first use in North Africa. Insofar as is known, no M1 bazookas were used in the Pacific. The 2nd Marine Division was to have received 243 M1A1 bazookas in time for the brutal Tarawa assault in November 1943, but while the shipment arrived in Wellington, New Zealand, it was misplaced and the Marines had to seize an island bristling with more than 500 pillboxes, bunkers, and dugouts without the benefit of the weapon. The division's after-action report stated the bazooka would have been invaluable and should equip all future landing forces.

There was some very limited use of the bazooka by the 1st Corps Experimental Rocket Detachment in June 1943 in the Northern Solomons. It conducted field and combat testing of the bazooka and other rocket systems. Yet both the Army and Marines' first use of bazookas in the Pacific was on New Britain in December 1943, when the 112th Cavalry Regiment (serving dismounted as infantry) landed at Arawa on the south-central coast and the 1st Marine Division landed at Cape Gloucester on the island's west end. This first Pacific demonstration of the bazooka was unimpressive. There was no armor to fight and Japanese bunkers were made of damp earth and soggy coconut logs, which absorbed much of the blast. The persistent rain and humidity seriously affected the bazooka's electrical system. The short ranges caused by the dense jungle also limited their use. These same problems persisted during subsequent Army operations on New Guinea's north coast.

The GIs' tank-killer (previous pages)

Germany, 1945. Infantry were being issued the new 2.36in M9 bazooka to replace the M1A1. This much-improved model offered a two-piece, breakdown launcher tube, better sight, 50yd-longer effective range, and a more reliable and lethal high-explosive antitank (HEAT) rocket. Even with a round offering greater penetration, the most effective hits were still on a tank's sides and rear. With the growing Allied use of shaped-charge munitions, especially man-portable rocket launchers, rifle grenades, and hand-delivered mines, in March 1943 the Germans began adding skirting (*Schürzen*) to many tanks and assault guns. This was not actually an armor plate, but sheet metal 0.2in thick. Thicker 0.31in skirting was added to turrets. GIs called the skirts "bazooka pants." In September, 1944 wire-mesh skirting (*Drahtgeflecht Schürzen*) replaced the sheet metal of the same profile. It was lighter, less costly, and just as effective. Either type of skirting caused shaped-charge rounds to detonate a short distance from the hull/turret and dissipated the penetrating blast to a degree. In this instance the loader of a two-man bazooka crew attacking a PzKpfw IV Ausf. H (aka Mk IV) carries two M6 rocket bags, each holding three rounds. The bazooka's light weight allowed crews to stalk tanks through dense vegetation, broken ground, and urban rubble. This tactical ability allowed them to avoid any accompanying infantry, evade the tanks' machine guns, and find suitable concealed firing positions enabling them to attack AFVs from favorable angles and take advantage of vulnerabilities. Such an approach was, of course, not always effective. Tank-stalking was a dangerous endeavor no matter how well trained and experienced the crew was. In the left foreground are discarded crates for 8.8cm *Panzerschreck* R.Pz.Gr.4322 rockets, used in the German "bazooka."

A Marine gunnery sergeant sights an M1A1 bazooka, November 1943. The Marine Corps' first use of the bazooka was on New Britain at Cape Gloucester in December 1943. The Army's first use of the bazooka in the Pacific was also on New Britain. His left hand grips the tube – the forward handgrip had been deleted from the M1A1. He could also place his left hand on the bottom of the handgrip for more support. Both positions were acceptable. (Tom Laemlein/Armor Plate Press)

Bazookas proved to be more effective during the February 1944 Marshall Islands assault by the 4th Marine Division and 7th Infantry Division. These were short-term operations and while used effectively against concrete pillboxes, the bazookas did not have the opportunity to prove their full worth.

The bazooka's opportunity to shine came in June 1944, with the opening of the Marianas campaign. The Marines were still using the M1A1 and the Army divisions now had the M9. Saipan, Tinian, and Guam were riddled with pillboxes and caves. The bazookas were therefore put to good use. On June 17 at 0330hrs, the Japanese 48th Tank Regiment with 37 tanks and 500 infantry counterattacked the 2nd Marine Division. Backed by artillery, Marine Sherman tanks, 37mm antitank guns, and bazookas opened fire, knocking out 24 tanks and killing 300 infantry. It was the largest tank-vs-tank engagement in the Pacific. Bazookas contributed their share of kills. There were so many claims of tank kills that they totaled some three times the number of tanks involved. There were smaller tank engagements through the campaign and there were also minor tank engagements on Tinian and Guam.

Pvt Thomas Baker of the 105th Infantry Regiment, 27th Infantry Division, over a three-week period on Saipan in June and July 1944 demonstrated repeated acts of valor, including while armed with a bazooka. He obtained an M9 bazooka and dashed alone to within 100yd of an enemy strongpoint. Despite heavy rifle and machine-gun fire he fully exposed himself and knocked out a strongpoint with repeated rocket hits, allowing his company to assault the ridge. This was the first of a series of individual acts of courage in which Baker killed dozens of the enemy, until he was seriously wounded and allowed himself to be trapped so he could cover the withdrawal of his comrades. With eight pistol rounds he killed eight enemy soldiers before meeting his death.

Both the 1st Marine (M1A1 equipped) and 81st Infantry (M9) Divisions made good use of bazookas on Peleliu from September through November 1944. The island's central hills were a chaotic jumble of ridges, outcroppings, gorges, crags, and sinkholes riddled with casemates, blockhouses, bunkers, pillboxes, and fortified caves, all mutually supporting. Bazookas were often the only supporting weapons capable of being moved into position – albeit with great difficulty – to suppress enemy positions.

Pfc Robert Montgomery of the 5th Marines, 1st Marine Division, was separated from his company during an assault on a hill. The company was pinned down by artillery, mortar, and machine-gun fire. Montgomery observed a dug-in 75mm gun about to take his unit under direct fire. He closed to within 50yd and fired nine rockets from an exposed position, wiping out the entire crew and destroying the gun by penetrating its shield. He received the Bronze Star. Montgomery was killed on Okinawa leading an assault platoon armed with bazookas and flamethrowers, and received the Silver Star posthumously for his actions there.

The Marines first used the M9 bazooka on Iwo Jima from February to March 1945. As on Peleliu the bazooka was the only weapon that could be moved into position to engage enemy fortifications on the volcanic island. Pfc Douglas Jacobson of the 23rd Marines, 4th Marine Division, was presented the Medal of Honor after grabbing an M9 bazooka from his fallen gunner as his platoon attacked a heavily fortified hill. In sequence he destroyed two machine-gun nests and a 20mm gun position, neutralized a large blockhouse, then a concrete bunker, knocked out a dug-in position, and then destroyed six more rifle positions. After his company occupied the strongpoint, he went to assist an adjacent company. They too were stalled, and Jacobson knocked out a pillbox, a dug-in enemy tank firing on a supporting Marine tank, and then a blockhouse, allowing the company to secure its objective. In a matter of hours Jacobson had killed approximately 75 of the enemy and destroyed 16 positions. It was a good day's work for a single bazooka-man.

Both the Army and Marines employed the M9 on Okinawa, where they encountered little armor, but seemingly endless fortifications. Some new weapons were tested as competitors of the bazooka in the bunker-busting role: the 4.2in M4 direct-fire recoilless mortar and the 57mm T15E9 and 75mm T21 recoilless rifles. While the M4 was effective, it was a heavy tripod-mounted weapon, as was the 75mm recoilless rifle. The 75mm was 5ft long, the same as a 3.5in bazooka, but it weighed 48.6lb, almost four times more than the bazooka, and had extremely poor armor penetration – 2.5in. These first-generation recoilless rifles were relatively ineffective for antitank use as they used spin-stabilized HEAT rounds rather than fin-stabilized non-rotating projectiles. Rotating projectiles dissipated the shaped-charge blast through centrifugal force causing a broader and shallower penetrating blast.

Bazookas proved valuable in the Philippines where the Japanese deployed armor to some extent on the larger islands. The entire Japanese 2nd Tank Division fought on northern Luzon, albeit often using its tanks simply as dug-in "pillboxes." Besides killing tanks, bazookas were critical for defeating fortifications and defended buildings in the many towns and cities. The 503rd Parachute Infantry Regiment jumped onto Corregidor with M9A1s for fortification reduction and the 6th Ranger Battalion destroyed six tanks with bazookas during the Cabanatuan prison camp raid on Luzon.[2]

Another bazooka-wielding Medal of Honor recipient was Pfc Dirk Vlug of the 126th Infantry, 32nd Infantry Division, on Leyte in December 1944. Several Japanese tanks attacked a US roadblock on the Ormoc Road. Leaving a protected position armed with an M9 bazooka and six rockets, he rushed under tank main gun and machine-gun fire to meet the two lead tanks. He destroyed the first tank with one round, killing the entire crew. As the second tank's crew dismounted to attack Vlug, he shot one with his pistol forcing the other two back into their tank, which he promptly destroyed with another rocket. He circled to the flank and destroyed a third tank. Repositioning under fire, he knocked out the fourth and then hit the last tank, forcing it to crash down a steep embankment.

Two Marines check out an M9 bazooka on Iwo Jima, February 1945. Iwo Jima saw the Marine Corps' first use of the M9. The bar sight is set for its maximum of 600yd range. The back-blast would kick up a considerable amount of Iwo Jima's fine black volcanic sand. (Tom Laemlein/ Armor Plate Press)

While there were initial problems – some serious, with the first bazookas – the weapon proved to be extremely useful and deadly. They and their rockets were improved and provided troops with a reasonably effective, highly portable, lightweight tank- and bunker-killer. The 1944 *Report of the New Weapons Board* summed up the bazooka:

2.36" Rocket and Launchers

a. The feeling existed in both theaters [Europe and Italy] that the 2.36" rocket had been oversold. This feeling was accompanied by questions as to the effectiveness and accuracy of the 2.36" HEAT rocket. In view of this, the Board incorporated a 2.36" rocket show into each demonstration [given to unit officers]. The entire renovation of the original launcher [M1] and rocket [M7] was explained. The explanation included a description of the new wagon-wheel pulpit trap and its function [M6A1]. To demonstrate the safety of the [M1A1] launcher, a launcher which had had two rocket motors exploded within the wire-wrapped portion was exhibited. Two bazookas were then fired at a tank at an 80yd range. Amazement was expressed by many spectators at the accuracy and results which were obtained by inexperienced rocket operators. Each demonstration included the firing of six rounds, and it was the exception when there were less than six hits.

b. Many types of eye and face protection have been improvised by combat troops using the 2.36" rocket launcher. Some enlisted men use

[2] See Gordon Rottman, *The Cabanatuan Prison Raid: The Philippines 1945*, Osprey Raid 3, Oxford: Osprey (2009)

motorcycle goggles. Others used a modified gasmask, the bottom of which has been cut away; still others use the gasmask as issued. One officer stated that he had obtained excellent results with the use of a plexiglass shield attached to the end of the launcher. Some enlisted men are using celluloid or plastic face shields. Some shields are made to cover the eyes only, whereas others cover the entire face. It was reported that the frustum of a cone [truncated cone], which had been placed on some launchers, does not serve its purpose. It is believed that this problem should be solved completely and that an item which will afford ample face protection at all temperatures should be developed and issued without delay.

c. Brig. Gen. Arthur H. Rogers, formerly of the North African theater, reported that early in the Italian campaign a number of the 2.36" rockets carried by his men failed to function. Gen. Rogers stated that these rockets had been carried in ammunition carriers, which hold eight rockets, four in back and four in front [mortar vests]. He said that these rockets had been carried fins up, with the fins exposed, and that undoubtedly they had been dragged through mud and water. It was Gen. Rogers' opinion that the rockets which failed to function failed because moisture entered the motor, although he was not certain that the electrical connection had not been loosened. It is believed that in view of this report the 2.36" rocket should be given thorough proof tests for resistance against moisture. Gen. Rogers also told the Board of a new way in which he employed the bazookas of his organization during the early part of the Italian campaign. He said that he formed bazooka hunting teams. These teams employed 10 to 12 bazookas in one group and went hunting at night. He said that their operation was most successful and that the ambushing of stationary German combat vehicles in this fashion was relatively simple. He spoke very highly of the 2.36" rocket and launcher.

A bazooka team in Belgium in January 1945 prepares a meal from 10-in-1 group rations. Their M9 launcher is broken down. It could be carried loaded when broken down, but this was not recommended and seldom occurred. (Tom Laemlein/Armor Plate Press)

Jongbu area, April,1951. 25th Infantry Division soldiers fire an M20 bazooka with the bipod removed (the bipod slide is still attached), a common practice to reduce the weight, as many felt the bipod was unnecessary. The dust kicked up by the back-blast is still settling. (Tom Laemlein/Armor Plate Press)

THE KOREAN WAR – BAZOOKA FAILURES AND SUCCESSES

The 3.5in M20 "super bazooka" had been standardized in late 1945, put into limited production in 1948, and issued only to select units in West Germany and the United States. MacArthur's Far East Command, mainly involved in the peaceful occupation of Japan, incorrectly assessed that no significant armor threat existed in the theater. When North Korean forces stormed across the 38th Parallel on June 25, 1950, however, they were accompanied by at least 120 Soviet-built T34/85 tanks (North Korea possessed 258). These were concentrated in the west to support the main attack. The battalion-size Task Force Smith hurriedly dispatched from Japan by the 24th Infantry Division was the first American force to engage the North Koreans. The 400-man force established a blocking position near Osan on July 4 in an effort to halt the advancing North Koreans after they seized Seoul and routed South Korean forces.

The unit's only antitank weapons were six M9A1 bazookas, two 75mm M20 recoilless rifles, and six HEAT rounds for a 105mm howitzer sited to cover the road. Five other howitzers provided indirect fire. In the morning of the 5th, eight T-34s unaccompanied by infantry approached and were taken under fire. The artillery barrage had no effect and while the 75mm recoilless rifles made direct hits at long range, they caused no damage. As the tanks approached the infantry positions they were struck at long range by the bazookas, again with no effect. Close-range fire was little better. 2nd Lt Ollie Connor claims to have fired 22 rockets from 15yd at a T-34's rear, supposedly a vulnerable spot, with most being misfires, duds, or ricochets.[3] The direct-fire howitzer destroyed one tank and

---

[3] The T-34/85's front hull armor was 1.85in, sides 1.77in, turret front 2.36in, turret sides 2in, rear 1.77in. The high degree of armor slope was more the cause of the 2.36in missile's failure than the armor's thickness.

damaged another with its HEAT rounds. Switching to HE, it destroyed another, plus one tank was halted by an indirect howitzer hit. The remaining four tanks pressed on through the American position.

An hour later 25 more tanks, again unaccompanied by infantry, appeared. Indirect artillery halted one and damaged three. This unorganized column knocked out the direct-fire howitzer and caused some Americans to flee. The tanks continued southward. Then before noon a 6-mile-long truck column carrying two infantry regiments arrived with three tanks in the lead. It appears the earlier tank formations were not in contact with the infantry, who were unaware of the US roadblock. At 1,000yd the Americans opened up with rifle, machine-gun, mortar, and artillery fire, but communications between the infantry and artillery broke down and the artillery was largely ineffective. A few trucks were hit and the North Koreans were forced to dismount. They began deploying large forces on the flanks to encircle the Americans, then attacked supported by mortars, artillery, and the three tanks. After holding out for two hours, the Americans withdrew, some organized, some fleeing. Some 250 made it south to join up with other units. About 150 were killed, captured, and wounded. The 2.36in was not up to the task of stopping the enemy armor.

The 1st Marine Division landed at Inch'on on September 15 and struck toward Seoul. Pfc Walter Monegan of the 1st Marines, 1st Marine Division, was dug-in on a hill overlooking the Seoul Highway when six T-34/85 tanks attacked and threatened to break through the battalion. During the

Bunker-busting bazookas (previous pages)

While proving effective against North Korean-manned Soviet-made T-34/85 tanks, and absolutely devastating against the other primary North Korean AFV, the 76mm SU-76M assault gun, the 3.5in M20 "super bazooka" was also a lethal anti-bunker weapon. Bazookas were used far more in this role than as tank killers. The "three-point-five" offered adequate accuracy out to 300yd, but was very accurate to 150yd, its rated effective range. Most bunker engagements were at shorter ranges, and it was easy for a bazooka gunner to slam a round through a firing port. The difficult part was to avoid the bunker's field of fire, as well as fire from adjacent mutually supporting bunkers on ridge and hilltops. In order to blind supporting bunkers and other firing positions, white phosphorus (WP) M30 rockets were fired, as seen at the upper bunker here. They not only created instant dense white smoke screens when they burst, but showered burning gobs and particles of burning WP into open-topped fighting positions, causing casualties and driving out the enemy. Burning WP is sticky and smears if one tries to wipe it off. Bursting radius was about 25yd. The M28 HEAT rocket was loaded with almost 3lb of Composition B, three times more explosive than the old 2.36in rocket. Comp B has a relative effectiveness of 1.35 compared to TNT, rated at 1.00. The 81mm mortar light high-explosive (HE) projectile held only 1.22lb of TNT, making the 3.5in HEAT round essentially a demolition charge when attacking field fortifications. The HEAT round could easily penetrate four layers of sandbags and even more logs. At this time, the rifle platoon's weapons squad possessed a bazooka team with a rocket gunner, assistant gunner (both with M1911A1 pistols), and two ammunition bearers (one with an M1 rifle, one with an M2 carbine). In mid-1952, the weapons squad received a second .30cal M1919A6 machine gun and the bazooka team was transferred to the platoon headquarters.

pre-dawn attack, Monegan left his position with his 3.5in M20 bazooka and moved to less than 50yd of the lead tank. He hit the tank and then shot the sole crew survivor with his carbine. He fired two more rockets at the following tanks, missing them but succeeding in disorganizing their advance, enabling Marine tanks to engage. However, North Korean infantry and tanks were able to bypass the position and pressed their attack. Monegan took his bazooka forward and knocked out two more tanks while completely exposed to heavy fire. He moved to tackle another tank that was turning to flee, and was himself fatally hit by enemy fire.

The 2.36in M9A1 equipped both US and South Korean forces at the war's beginning, although it was scheduled to be replaced by the 3.5in

A well-used 3.5in M20 bazooka is fired by a Marine using a "non-standard" firing position. Both the gunner and loader are armed with .45cal M1911A1 pistols, standard armament for Marine bazooka crewmen. (Tom Laemlein/Armor Plate Press)

Marines man a hillside outpost overlooking a valley, armed with a .50cal M2 machine gun and a 3.5in M20 rocket launcher. Additional rockets are laid out on a canvas tarp to the left. Owing to the adverse effects of prolonged exposure to direct sunlight on rocket propellant, it was recommended they be kept under cover. (© Bettmann/Corbis)

M20. Pre-Korean War TO&E authorized the 3.5in for rifle companies, while headquarters, service, and support units still had the 2.36in for self-defense. The smaller caliber weapons would eventually be replaced by the 3.5in. A point that is misunderstood in regards to the issue of the 3.5in is that it is often incorrectly reported that production and even development did not commence until after the 2.36in was found ineffective against the T-34/85. The 3.5in was actually in limited production by the outbreak of war and fielding had begun to units in West Germany and the US. Actually, only the first three Army divisions – 1st Cavalry and 24th and 25th Infantry – deploying to Korea from Japan, were armed with the 2.36in. The five subsequent Army divisions, separate regiments, and the Marines – in other words, all units arriving after the beginning of August – went to Korea with the 3.5in. Units arriving in Korea during July lacked the 3.5in, but had it within weeks. A small number of super bazookas were flown to Korea even earlier and used by the 24th Infantry Division from July 18, 1950 during the battle of Taejon, where eight T-34s were knocked out on the first day of their use. In August the early arriving units still armed with M9A1 bazookas sent their rifle-platoon rocket gunners to the rear to be trained and qualified on the new weapon by Infantry School training teams accompanying the replacement 3.5in launchers. As the new bazookas operated almost identically to the M9A1, the gunners quickly returned to their units with the lethal new launchers and basic loads of ammunition.

At one point the USA withdrew 3.5in bazookas from South Korean divisions, replacing them with the 2.36in because so many launchers were being captured and turned on UN tanks. The 2.36in was ineffective against the US M26 Pershing heavy tank, although it could cause problems for the still-numerous M4A3 Sherman medium tank. In addition, the South Koreans seldom faced T-34 tanks. As the Koreans became more tactically competent and experienced, the 3.5in was reissued. The 3.5in was also issued to all other UN forces fighting in Korea.

North Korea lost 239 T-34/85 tanks and 74 SU-76M 76mm assault guns. Most of these were killed by UN fighter-bombers and tanks, but bazookas took their fair share. From November 1951, the Korean War evolved into static positional warfare and few enemy tanks were encountered. The Chinese had a couple of hundred tanks, but they and the North Koreans held them in reserve, seldom committing even small numbers. The 3.5in proved to be very effective against bunkers and other fortified positions, and was also important because the 57mm, 75mm and 105mm recoilless rifles had poor armor and log/sandbag penetration.

FIRING THE 3.5in M20 SERIES BAZOOKAS

The M20/M20B1 bazookas operated almost identically to the 2.36in M9A1; only differences will be described here. The gunner had to be aware of what type of firing mechanism a particular bazooka had equipped. On early M20s, the "Safe" position was up and on later ones it was down, to include all M20A1s. Before the rocket was loaded, a

shorting clip was removed from the contact ring encircling the fins and then the warhead inserted in the tube. The arming clip was removed from the motor and the rocket slid fully in. The lead wire was then extended and wrapped around the connector coil.

The M20A1 was significantly modified by deleting the connector coils and the connector clamp atop the breech. These were replaced by a connector-latch group assembly on top of the breech. This box-like housing had a control handle in the forward end. The lever was placed in the down position for loading. The rocket was loaded in the same manner as described above, but the lead wire did not have to be attached. The control handle was raised rearward and the weapon was ready to fire after the gunner set the safety to "Fire."

There were a series of actions and commands given to ensure crew efficiency and safety. When ready to load, the gunner would remove his hand from the trigger, tap the loader with his right hand and command, "Load." During initial training the gunner placed his right hand atop his helmet to prevent inadvertent trigger pulling. The loader repeated, "Load," and loaded a rocket. When loaded and after checking that the back-blast area was clear, he tapped the gunner and said, "Up." The gunner placed his fingers back on the trigger, aimed, and fired.

The M20 series bazookas delivered somewhat more back-blast flash and smoke than the 2.36in, but still no muzzle flash, although there was some smoke expelled. The author had occasion to fire only a few rounds from an M20A1B1 during infantry training and Special Forces weapons training. There was absolutely no recoil, but the sudden absence of a 9lb rocket

The assistant gunner of a Marine rocket team loads an M28 HEAT rocket into an M20 launcher in November 1951. Often the loader was more exposed than the gunner during the loading process. This is one instance in which the weapon was actually fired from the seldom-used bipod and monopod. Note that after frequent firing the paint is worn off the inside of the muzzle-blast protector. (Tom Laemlein/Armor Plate Press)

caused the launcher to shift or jump slightly. The back-blast of the 57mm and 90mm recoilless rifles was brutal compared to the bazooka's.

The 3.5in, owing to its more powerful rocket, created a much larger back-blast cone than the 2.36in. Instead of a 20ft-wide 20ft-deep cone, the 3.5in had three danger zones. Zone A – 25×25yd – had to be clear of all personnel, ammunition, materiel, and flammables. Zone B – inclusive of Zone A, 50×50yd – should have been clear of personnel, ammunition, materiel, and flammables unless under cover. Zone C – inclusive of Zones A and B, 75×75yd – was an additional safety area used in training only. Besides the considerable blast, there was danger from expelled lead wires and nozzle protector caps, and blasted gravel and other ground debris. Instructors demonstrated the deadly effects of the back-blast by stacking empty ammunition crates a few yards behind the launcher and firing it, with the crates being blown to splinters.

CREWING AND ALLOCATION OF 3.5in BAZOOKAS

After World War II the Army rifle platoon received a weapons squad armed with a bazooka and a .30cal M1919A6 light machine gun. The bazooka crew consisted of the rocket gunner, assistant rocket gunner, and two ammunition bearers. In May 1952, when a second machine gun was added, the bazooka team was reassigned to the platoon headquarters. In Korea, after the shift to static warfare and on account of the scarcity of tanks, many units made little or no use of the bazooka. Many soldiers stated they never saw one, or seldom did. Only 15–25 percent of units made habitual use of it. Many preferred the three 57mm recoilless rifles assigned to the company. Even though that weapon was heavier and had limited effect on bunkers, its ammunition was lighter and it was longer-ranged – important in the hills – and more accurate than the bazooka. While the 57mm was much heavier than the 3.5in, the lighter rounds allowed more ammunition to be carried and that was an acceptable tradeoff. Some units preferred an additional machine gun over the bazooka. Still others recommended the bazooka for raids and daylight patrols, as it was effective against bunkers and useful for reconnaissance by fire.

This allocation remained standard until 1958, when the Pentomic concept was implemented.[4] The weapons squad retained two machine guns,

---

[4] The Pentomic structure of 1958–62 unsuccessfully attempted to field a division optimized for the nuclear battlefield. The Pentomic division consisted of five battle groups (enlarged, self-sustaining battalions) rather than three regiments.

but the bazooka team was reassigned to the squad, now with a gunner, assistant, and one ammunition bearer. In addition, there were two bazookas in the company headquarters and two in the weapon platoon headquarters for self-defense. In the early 1960s, the Army again reorganized. Now the weapons squad had two 3.5in launchers with two-man crews and a single ammunition bearer shared between them, but at the same time the 90mm M67 recoilless rifle began replacing the bazooka. The 3.5in was still assigned to units for self-defense without dedicated crews – one in the company headquarters and two in the weapons platoon – but in the mid-1960s the Light Antitank Weapon (LAW) would replace the bazooka in this role too.

A Marine crew prepares to fire an M20A1B1 rocket launcher, which is a 1952 field-modified version of the M20B1 – note it retains the M20B1's monopod grip integral to the shoulder rest, but the monopod itself was removed in 1957. (Tom Laemlein/Armor Plate Press)

The Marines concentrated their 3.5in launchers in the rifle company weapons platoon's assault section, with six weapons with three-man crews. In Vietnam, the bazookas were often placed in storage, but some units made at least limited use of them for bunker-busting and occasional city fighting. Army units arriving in Vietnam armed with the 3.5in or the 90mm recoilless rifle usually did the same.

Carrying bulky 9lb 3.5in rockets was problematic. There was a web-strap rocket carrier with shoulder sling for carrying two rockets. The loader and ammunition bearers each carried two of these, but they were little used. The 1961 manual called for the gunner to carry one rocket and the loader six in packing tubes (approximately 60lb). Mostly they were carried in a standard backpack or strapped under the top flap of aluminum-frame rucksacks or tied together in bundles. More realistically each man carried only two rockets.

AFTER THE KOREAN WAR

The M20A1B1 remained as the primary platoon antitank weapon until replaced by the 90mm recoilless rifle in the mid-1960s. It saw some use in Vietnam, by the Marines somewhat more than the Army, and also to a limited degree by the Army of the Republic of Vietnam (ARVN). Martin J. Dockery describes his experiences with the bazooka as an ARVN advisor in 1962–63 in *Lost in Translation: Vietnam: A Combat Advisor's Story* (Presidio Press, 2003):

> The second-most dangerous place on an operation was anywhere near the soldier who carried the 3.5in rocket launcher. This shoulder-fired weapon was a 50in-long metal tube that fired an explosive-filled rocket. It was most effective against fortifications and vehicles. A second soldier carried the rockets and served as the loader. In order

to avoid wounding friendly soldiers, this weapon had to be used with utmost care. The loader's tap on the head of the soldier aiming the bazooka signaled that the weapon was loaded and no friendly soldiers were in the back-blast area. When the weapon was fired, metal bits and other debris were propelled sixty feet backward in a thirty-degree arc.

Captain Beng [ARVN battalion CO] kept the 3.5-inch rocket launcher in the rear with him so he could direct its use and lessen the possibility of losing it to the Viet Cong. He would authorize its use if the request was sufficiently urgent to convince him that it was really needed. The two-man team, amidst vocal encouragement from the soldiers they passed, would scamper up the trail, one carrying the rocket launcher and the other lugging a bag of rockets. The soldiers they encountered did not know where the firing position would be, but they all knew they could be wounded by the back-blast so they sought protection. Shooting at the enemy stopped as the battalion soldiers sought safer positions. When the launcher team arrived where it was needed, often conflicting orders or just general confusion caused the team to point the weapon one way, then another way. Each change in direction changed the location of the back-blast area and caused soldiers to rush to a safer place. As a result, there was no covering fire for the soldier who had to expose himself to fire the rocket on target. At times the excitement and fear were so great that the rocket was fired before everyone was out of the back-blast area and before a worthy target was selected. Early in my tour I was nearly wounded by just such an incident. A soldier close to me received a deep facial gash. I felt the heat and the blast, but was unhurt.

The French used both the 2.36in M9A1 and 3.5in M20A1 in Indochina and Algeria. The M20A1 remained the French platoon antitank weapon until the early 1970s, when the bazooka-like 89mm F1 LRAC was adopted. The Viet Minh made very crude copies of bazookas using 2.36in rockets. Many M9A1s had been supplied to the Nationalist Chinese during World War II and they were used by both sides in the 1946–50 Chinese Civil War.

The famous revolutionary Ernesto "Che" Guevara, in *Guerrilla Warfare* (1961), stated:

> The bazooka is a heavy weapon that can be used by the guerrilla band because of its easy portability and operation. Naturally, it will be a weapon taken from the enemy. The bazooka is ideal for firing on armored vehicles, and even on unarmored vehicles that are loaded with troops, and for taking small military bases of few men in a short time; but it is important to point out that not more than three shells per man can be carried, and this only with considerable exertion.

Of course in later insurgencies the Soviet RPG became the shoulder-fired rocket launcher of choice.

Most British Commonwealth forces (UK, Australia, Canada) used the 3.5in as the platoon antitank weapon until adopting the Carl Gustav L14A1 in the mid-1960s. They referred to the M20 and M20A1 as the M20 Mk I and Mk II, respectively. Other countries using the 3.5in M20 series included: Argentina, Austria, Bolivia, Brazil, Burma, Cuba, India, Japan, Luxembourg, Morocco, Nationalist China (Taiwan), Pakistan, Philippines, Portugal, Rhodesia, South Africa, South Korea, Sweden, Thailand, Tunisia, Turkey, and West Germany. It also saw use in a number of small countries in Latin America.

British Royal Marines man a hastily constructed sangar (piled rocks) defensive position on Mutla Ridge in Kuwait during the 1961 confrontation with Iraq. They are armed with an M20 Mk I (US M20) bazooka. The M20 Mk I and the M20 Mk II (US M20A1) remained in Commonwealth service into the 1970s. (© Bettmann/Corbis)

IMPACT
The bazooka's legacy

"Armed with this weapon, the individual foot soldier possessed, for the first time, the means whereby he could, singlehandedly, do battle with a tank" (Lt Gen Levin H. Campbell, Chief of Ordnance, 1943). While any weapon has its flaws and limitations, the bazooka was instrumental in achieving the final victory in World War II. It was relatively successful in its primary role – killing tanks. It at least improved the foot-mobile soldier's chances of destroying enemy armor, and was certainly superior to the infantry alternatives. It also gave him a weapon that greatly extended his reach and killing power. The bazooka simply gave infantrymen an easily portable means of direct-firing an HE round at a variety of targets within 200yd. They were commonly used against light AFVs, soft-skin vehicles, defended buildings, field fortifications, caves, crew-served weapons, troops in the open, and snipers among others. Probably one of the most significant oversights with the bazooka, however, was the failure to develop an HE round optimized for attacking bunkers and fortifications. Such a round would also have been more effective for antipersonnel use than the HEAT.

The imagination of the American fighting men was demonstrated by the many types of targets attacked by the bazooka, and innovative methods of its use. As we have seen, they were occasionally mounted on vehicles, aircraft, and watercraft, usually in multiple mounts. A method was even found to launch 2.36in rockets from their shipping tube – buried in the ground at an angle – for indirect area fire. The 3.5in rocket was adopted as an off-route mine to attack the more vulnerable tank flanks.

One important attribute of the bazooka was that it was so readily available, owing to its low cost and short manufacturing time. In 1942 the Army infantry division was assigned 557, the armored division 607, and the airborne division 182, allocations that were increased to 445 in the airborne division in 1944 and 567 by the war's end. The Marines issued fewer owing to a very limited armor threat in the Pacific theater. In 1942 the Marine division was authorized 132 bazookas. This was somewhat increased in 1943 when they became more available, but they were later reduced to 172 in 1944 and 153 in 1945. There were still sufficient numbers available for their main role in the Pacific, defeating pillboxes and caves.

There is little doubt that the bazooka was considered a threat by the Germans. The presence of the bazooka reinforced the need for accompanying infantry to protect tanks from close-in attacks. In an effort to counter the shaped charge delivered by the bazooka and similar weapons, the Germans attached thin sheet-steel or wire-mesh panels to the sides of many tanks and assault guns, to protect the hull sides and upper suspension system. The same measures were sometimes installed around the sides and rear of tank turrets. The 0.16–0.24in-thick steel skirting was installed on new-production tanks and assault guns from March 1943, and the lighter *Drahtgeflecht Schürzen* (wire-mesh skirting) was introduced on PzKpfw IV tanks in September 1944. It has been reported that the sheet-metal panels were installed solely to help protect the tanks from Soviet antitank rifles; they appear to have caused the 14.5mm bullets to fragment or "keyhole" (turn sideways) and fail to penetrate the main armor. They were, however, actually intended to protect against shaped-charge projectiles. The wire-mesh skirting offered no protection from antitank rifle bullets.

An Aggressor antitank team prepares to attack an American force with an M20A1B1 bazooka, early 1960s. The connector box and arming lever can be seen atop the breech. The forest-green-uniformed Aggressor was the "maneuver enemy" used in training exercises from 1953 to 1976, when it was replaced by the Opposing Forces (OPFOR) concept. (Texas Military Forces Museum)

INFLUENCE ON POSTWAR WEAPONS

The bazooka demonstrated the practicality of the man-portable, shoulder-fired rocket launcher as an antitank weapon. Besides leading to the development of the German *Panzerschreck*, the bazooka was to influence similar postwar weapons. Among these were the Belgian 83mm and 100mm RL-83 and RL-100 *Blindicide,* Spanish 89mm (firing US 3.5in) Mod 65 *bazuca,* and French LARC 89mm F1 *Lance-Roquette Anti-Char* (antitank rocket launcher). These weapons were not much better than the M20 series bazooka, but were largely interim weapons until advanced wire-guided antiarmor missiles appeared in the 1970s.

In 1951 Communist China reverse-engineered the M20 to produce the 87mm Type 51 rocket launcher, which saw service in Korea from 1952 as well as limited use in Vietnam. It is often called a 90mm, rounding off the caliber, and some claim that it could fire US rockets, but Chinese rockets could not be fired in US launchers. This was not true – they were interchangeable, even though it was recommended not to use Chinese rockets for safety reasons. In the 1950s Brazil modified the M20A1B1 as the 89mm Hydroar *bazuca* with modifications made by Hydroar SA Industria Metalurgica of São Paolo. The US-designed magneto handgrip was replaced by one with a solid-state firing circuit using two "AA" batteries (BA-3058).

A further offshoot of the bazooka was the shoulder-fired, single-shot, disposable rocket launcher emerging in the 1960s, the first being the

German soldiers unload crates of *Panzerfaust 60* antitank projectors. The *Panzerfaust* was a shoulder-fired single-shot recoilless projector launching a shaped-charge warhead. It was *not* a bazooka-type rocket launcher. (Texas Military Forces Museum)

US M72 LAW. It spawned at least a dozen similar weapons worldwide. The Soviet RPG-2 and RPG-7 antitank projectors were distantly influenced by the bazooka.[5]

THE 3.5in BAZOOKA'S REPLACEMENTS

The 3.5in bazooka was replaced in US service by three distinctly different weapons. As the Army's platoon antitank weapon, it was replaced by the 90mm (3.54in) M67 (T219E4) recoilless rifle on a one-for-one basis – two per platoon. Development of a 90mm recoilless rifle to replace the 3.5in bazooka had begun in the late 1940s and continued into the 1950s with the T149 and T184. The M67 was developed by the Midwest Research Institute in Kansas City, MO, and adopted in 1959.

Fielded in the early 1960s, the "ninety" offered marginal improvement over the bazooka and was considered too heavy. The muzzle and back-blast were uncomfortable for the crew. The M67 was a breech-loading shoulder-fired weapon weighing 37.5lb, three times more than the bazooka; its 53in length – 7in shorter than the bazooka– did not offset its heavier weight. It resurrected the M20's monopod and bipod to make the heavy weapon easier to fire from the prone position. The M67's M371E1 HEAT round was 5in longer and about a third of a pound heavier than the 3.5in rocket. It had an effective range of 440yd, not much better than the

3.5in, but its armor penetration was 14in under ideal conditions (2ft 6in for reinforced concrete). It also offered the XM590E1 antipersonnel round, which contained 2,400 dart-like flechettes. Operating with a shotgun-like effect, it sprayed flechettes up to 330yd. This round proved useful in Vietnam, but the M67 and its ammunition proved to be simply too heavy for the rugged terrain and brutal climate. Most units were allotted only one per platoon and it was seldom carried in the field. Some companies carried one, and others were sometimes heli-lifted to units if needed or were used for firebase defense. Many infantrymen in Vietnam never saw a 90mm. There was little need for the heavy weapon even as a bunker-buster.

The M67 was officially phased out in the mid-1970s in favor of the wire-guided Dragon antitank missile, but it remained in use into the early 1990s by the 1st and 2nd Ranger Battalions and the Berlin Brigade for

The 3.5in M20A1B1 was replaced as a self-defense weapon in headquarters and service units by the 66mm M72 LAW, adopted in 1963. It was widely used in Vietnam against bunkers, buildings, and snipers. It was effective against North Vietnamese Army (NVA) PT-76 and T-54 tanks, but required multiple hits. (US Army)

[5] See Gordon Rottman, *The Rocket Propelled Grenade*, Osprey Weapon 2, Oxford: Osprey (2009)

ABOVE

The far-too-heavy 90mm M67 recoilless rifle replaced the 3.5in M20A1B1 as the Army rifle platoon's antitank weapon in the early 1960s and was used into the 1970s, when it was replaced by the Dragon M47 wire-guided antiarmor missile. The 90mm remained in specialized roles into the 1990s and some have recently been used in Afghanistan. (US Army)

ABOVE RIGHT

In 1983 the US Marines began replacing the 3.5in as a bunker-busting assault and secondary antiarmor weapon with the 83mm Mk 153 Mod 0/1 Shoulder-Launched Multipurpose Assault Weapon (SMAW). The detachable rear tube doubles as a shipping container for the 83mm cartridge. The weapon is fitted (on the right side) with a 9mm Mk 8 Mod 0 spotting gun to improve first-round hit probability. (US Marine Corps)

close-range and urban combat. The 6th Infantry Division (Light) in Alaska also used it until the 1990s, as the Dragon experienced difficulties in extreme cold. In 2011 some 90mms were issued from reserve stocks to the 101st Airborne Division for attacking fortified compounds in Afghanistan.

While rifle platoons replaced the 3.5in bazooka with the M67, all other combat and support units retained 3.5in weapons for antitank defense. These units lacked dedicated bazooka crews and most units conducted little training on the launcher. For example, field artillery battalions had 20–30 depending on unit; engineer battalions 65, and signal battalions 26. In 1963 these self-defense bazookas and antitank rifle grenades began to be replaced by the 5.2lb M72 LAW. This was a 66mm (2.6in) single-shot, shoulder-fired, disposable rocket launcher. When the collapsible launcher unit was extended to fire it was 34.6in long, and 24.8in closed. The LAW was essentially a throwback to the original 2.36in bazooka, especially in that it was designed to deliver the heavy HEAT warhead of the M31 rifle grenade, not unlike the old problem with the M10 rifle grenade – a projectile too heavy to launch from a rifle. Its range was 220yd. Improved versions have since come into use.

The Marines phased out the 3.5in bazooka after Vietnam, retaining some in storage, but fielded the Dragon M47 wire-guided antitank missile in 1975. A complete Dragon with a 140mm (5.5in) missile weighed 37.5lb and had a 1,100yd range. The Army began to replace the 90mm M67 with the Dragon at the same time.

After Vietnam, the Marine assault section had M72A1/A2 LAWs and four-tube M202A1 Flash incendiary rocket launchers until 1984, when the 83mm (3.26in) Mk 153 Mod 0/1 Shoulder-Launched Multipurpose Assault Weapon (SMAW – pronounced "small") was introduced. The bazooka-like launcher is 54in long with its rocket loaded. Rockets are issued in special tubes that serve as both the shipping container and rear launch tube. It is provided with HE-dual-purpose and HE-antiarmor rounds with a 550yd range. Marine rifle companies possess six SMAWs in their assault section. The Army borrowed 150 SMAWs during *Desert Storm*.

The Swedish-designed Carl Gustav 84mm M2 recoilless rifle, in British terminology called the "L14A1 infantry anti-tank gun," was introduced into Commonwealth service in 1965. It replaced the 3.5in M20 Mk II, which remained in British inventories into the early 1970s. Carl Gustavs replaced many other countries' bazooka-like weapons.

CONCLUSION

When asked to name the four things that helped most to win World War II, Gen Dwight D. Eisenhower said, "The bazooka, the jeep, the atom bomb, and the C-47 Gooney Bird." The bazooka was ahead of its time, using new technology in the form of improved rocket motors and shaped-charge warheads. It appeared when it was needed to meet the armor threat, was low cost and could be rapidly produced, was simple to train on and operate, useable in multiple roles, and was sufficiently reliable. Its life would be limited owing to technological advances during and after the war – recoilless rifles and then wire-guided missiles. Introduced in 1942, the bazooka was phased out by the early 1970s, having served its purpose well.

Numerous soldiers received awards for valor for wielding the bazooka in combat. Among them were 15 soldiers and one Marine presented with the Medal of Honor in World War II, and one Marine in the Korean War. No records exist of how many tanks and other AFVs were knocked out by infantrymen using bazookas. Individual units did not even attempt to record such kills. It may have been only in the hundreds, but it was the wide range of other duties it provided, and its versatility, that proved the bazooka's worth.

GLOSSARY

BACK-BLAST: The explosive rearward blast of the bazooka's rocket upon ignition. Hazardous to personnel and equipment.

BARREL COUPLING: Threaded coupling and latch allowing the two barrel sections to be latched together for firing on the M9 series and M20 series bazookas.

BASE-DETONATING FUSE: Detonating fuse located at the rear end of the warhead. A base-detonating fuse's exploding impulse more effectively directs the main shaped charge's blast forward.

BAZOOKA: Common nickname for 2.36in and 3.5in antitank rocket launchers.

BIPOD: Folding two-legged ground mounting found on M20 bazookas.

BORESIGHTING: Procedure undertaken to align the sight with the axis of the bore.

BREECH GUARD: Conical-shaped rim protecting the breech and deflecting the back-blast on M18 and M20 series bazookas. On M1 series and M9 series bazookas it is a circular heavy wire frame guard.

CONNECTOR LATCH: Lever-like clamp atop the breech holding a loaded rocket in the barrel.

CONTACT SPRING: A pair of electrical contact posts and coiled springs on the rear portion of the barrel to which the rocket's ignition wire is attached for firing. Found on all bazookas except the unmodified M1, M20A1, and M20A1B1.

DANGER AREA: Cone-shaped area to the rear of a bazooka's breech that had to be clear of personnel, obstructions, and flammable materials when firing.

GRAZE EFFECT: When a projectile impacts at a low angle, such as into the ground or against sloped armor, it may not detonate as the fuse fails to function properly.

HANDGRIP: A pistol grip with the trigger, magneto, and safety on most models of bazooka.

MAGNETO: Component of the firing mechanism that generates an electric impulse when triggered to ignite the rocket motor.

MONOPOD: One-legged telescoping ground mount integral to the shoulder rest on M20 bazookas.

MUZZLE GUARD OR DEFLECTOR: Conical-shaped rim protecting the muzzle and deflecting any burning propellant on M9 series and M20 series bazookas.

NOSE CONE: Pointed or round-nosed windshield on the bazooka rocket's warhead. Aka ogive.

REINFORCING WIRE: Tightly wound piano wire wrapped around the rear portion of M1 series and M9 series bazookas to prevent the tube from bursting in event of a rocket motor exploding upon ignition.

ROCKET MOTOR: Bazooka rocket's propelling charge contained in the tailboom. It includes the base-detonating fuse, propellant igniter, electrical contacts, lead wire, and tailfins.

SAFETY BAND OR CLIP: Lever-released metal band securing the arming pin on the rocket motor.

TUBE: Rocket launcher barrel.

SHAPED CHARGE: An inverted cone-shaped high-explosive antitank (HEAT) warhead designed to penetrate armor. Aka hollow-charge or Munroe-effect.

STOCK: Wooden shoulder stock on the M1 series or metal shoulder rest on the M9 series and M20 series bazookas.

BIBLIOGRAPHY

Secondary sources

Canfield, Bruce N., *U.S. Infantry Weapons of World War II*, Lincoln, RI: Andrew Mowbray Publishing (1994)

Dockery, Martin J., *Lost in Translation: Vietnam: A Combat Advisor's Story*, Novato, CA: Presidio Press (2003)

Fleischer, Wolfgang, *Panzerfaust and other German Infantry Anti-tank Weapons*, Atglen, PA: Schiffer Publishing (1994)

Gander, Terry J., *The Bazooka: Hand-held Hollow-charge Anti-tank Weapons*, London: Parkgate Books (1998)

Green, Constance McLaughlin, Thomson, Harry C., and Roots, Peter C., *United States Army in World War II, The Technical Services, The Ordnance Department: Planning Munitions for War*, Washington, DC: US Government Printing Office (1955)

Guevara, Ernesto "Che," *Guerrilla Warfare*, Lincoln, NE: Bison Books (1998)

Miller, John A., *Men and Volts at War: The Story of General Electric in World War II*, New York, NY: McGraw-Hill (1947)

Reardon, Mark J., "The Bazooka" in Hoffman, Jon T. (ed.), *A History of Innovation: US Army Adaptation in War and Peace*, Washington, DC: Center for Military History (2009)

Thomson, Harry C. and Mayo, Lida, *United States Army in World War II, The Technical Services, The Ordnance Department: Procurement and Supply*, Washington, DC: US Government Printing Office (1960)

Military manuals

FM 23-30, *Hand and Rifle Grenades, Rocket, AT, HE, 2.36-inch* (February 1944)

FM 23-32, *3.5-inch Rocket Launcher* (December 1961)

TB 200-6, *Launcher, Rocket, AT, M1* (July 1942)

TM 2-294, *2.36-inch A.T. Rocket Launcher M1A1, 2.36-Inch Rocket Launchers M9 and M9A1* (June 1944; September, 1943 edition covered only M1A1. Change 1, June 1944, added M9 and M9A1)

TM 9-294, *2.36-inch Rocket Launchers M9, M9A1, and M18* (March 1946)

TM 9-297, *3.5-inch Rocket Launchers, M20 and M20B1* (August 1950)

TM 9-297A, *3.5-inch, Repeating Rocket Launcher M25 (T115E1) and Repeating Rocket Launcher Tripod Mount M77* (April 1951)

TM 9-1055-201-12, *Launchers, Rocket, 3.5-inch, M20A1 and M20A1B1* (October 1968_

(These and other manuals are available from Military/Info Publishing at <http://www.military-info.com>)

INDEX